TARTINE
BOOK Nº 3

DESIGN
JULIETTE CEZZAR

EDITORIAL DIRECTION
JESSICA BATTILANA

BREAD RESEARCH AND DEVELOPMENT
RICHARD HART

PASTRY RESEARCH AND DEVELOPMENT
LAURIE ELLEN PELLICANO

Library of Congress Cataloging-in-Publication Data available.

ISBN 978-1-4521-1430-9

Valrhona is a registered trademark of Valrhona S.A.
Kamut is a registered trademark of Kamut International, Ltd.
Maldon salt is a registered trademark of Maldon Crystal Salt Company Limited.

Manufactured in China.
Designed by Juliette Cezzar / e.a.d.

10 9 8 7 6 5 4 3 2 1

Chronicle Books LLC
680 Second Street
San Francisco, California 94107

www.chroniclebooks.com

TARTINE BOOK Nº 3
MODERN ANCIENT CLASSIC WHOLE

CHAD
ROBERTSON

CHRONICLE BOOKS
SAN FRANCISCO

For A

CONTENTS

Introduction

Working on the manuscript for my first book, *Tartine Bread,* was relatively straightforward. Published in late 2010, I told my story of learning to make bread, the people I learned from, and how I adapted techniques to achieve a wide range of results, all while working within a system of self-imposed strictures that were important to me. It was the story of searching for a singular loaf with an "old soul"—a traditional natural-leavened bread with all the qualities I loved bound together in one loaf. The basic recipe, which the entire premise of the book was built upon, detailed how to make the basic Tartine country loaf at home. This bread, and all its variations, tilted toward whiter flour and a lighter-flavored loaf.

The manuscript was delivered just as the home-baking movement seemed to reach critical mass. The young leaven method I have become known for, detailed in *Tartine Bread,* gave many home bakers and chefs the tools they needed to start making their own bread. Ambitious chefs were finally able to gain control over the quality, freshness, and character of the bread they wanted to serve with their food.

In Paris in the late 1970s, Lionel Poilâne famously began a dedicated effort to restore the heart and soul—*le vrai pain*—to the bread of his native France. This marked the beginning of a shift in taste back toward traditional country breads. A generation later, bakers around the world, myself included, were following Poilâne's lead. Poilâne did not traffic in baguettes; instead he was making a naturally leavened country *miche* (round loaf) using mostly high-extraction stone-milled wheat flour. Naturally leavened loaves are fermented slowly over a long period, resulting in breads with ancient depths of flavor that have been long forgotten. In doing so, he reintroduced the world to this revelation from the preindustrial French baking tradition.

While France is arguably the birthplace of the most elegant naturally leavened style, these breads are now more widely available than ever. We see natural-leavened bread produced in places where it didn't exist in the same way a decade ago, from London to Copenhagen, Stockholm to Tokyo, Lima to Tel Aviv.

In light of the current trend toward naturally leavened bread, it was clearly

time to force a creative push for our team at Tartine not only in our bread, but also with our classic Tartine pastry recipes. The year 2012 marked ten years since opening the bakery. Where could we take our recipes next? Could we make them taste even better while adding more nutrition? Respecting the foundation our reputation had been built on, the need to shift techniques and utilize new ingredients became the driving inspiration and challenge for this book.

For many years I had focused my efforts and exploration on the process of natural fermentation and how far one could push it while still maintaining balanced flavors and ending with an aesthetically pleasing loaf. Initially, I used a few types of flour: some white and some dark whole grains, with differing levels of protein (gluten). From the beginning, I had preferred to make my own flour blends in order to attain the qualities in a final loaf that I was after. Blending your own flours certainly gives more control, allowing the baker to fine-tune the crust and crumb, but much of the nuance in flavor was achieved by using different *preferments* (prefermented dough) in various stages and adjusting the times, temperatures, and flour percentages in the dough. With a few different types of flours to work with, I chose to focus on the transformative action of the leavens and the vastly different ways natural fermentation could add character to bread.

By the time I started making bread on my own, artisan baking in America was well under way. The Acme Bread Company

INTRODUCTION

on the West Coast and others on the East Coast had been making great bread for more than a decade. Our homegrown wheat flour had a reputation abroad as "strong flour," well suited for making good bread. It had high-quality gluten that allowed for optimum dough development and fermentation tolerance, resulting in bread with good volume, crust, and crumb (interior texture). But still, for most of us, wheat flours and, for that matter, bread were pretty black and white—or, rather, brown and white. The general perception of bread fell into two categories: white bread or darker brown whole-wheat bread (with few options in between). The first is made from white flour and the other from all or part whole-wheat flour.

Bakers use all sorts of flavorings for breads, such as nuts, seeds, dried fruit, herbs, and cheese. But I have always felt that relying on the addition of nongrain ingredients to add flavor to bread missed the heart of the matter. My focus would rely on the grains to bring the primary flavor— herbs, seeds, and other ingredients would complement this foundation.

Having lived in Northern California for the past twenty years, I've witnessed an incredible increase in the diversity of fruits and vegetables available to us. Years ago, we had a few varieties of tomatoes to choose from, a couple of different kales, and one or two types of broccoli; no one talked much about chicories, brassicas, and alliums, not to mention citrus, stone fruits, herbs, apples,

root vegetables, and beans (fresh and dried). Now we have dozens of varieties of each, all with distinct flavors. For cooks this is an inspiring resource. Why, then, have bakers in the States been working with only a few grains for so long?

The answer is not so simple. One must go deep into the history of farming in twentieth-century America, when the goal was to feed a rising population, and examine the shift from diversified farms to monocrop farming, aimed to achieve this goal in what seemed to be the most efficient fashion. As a result, the wheat-growing model was

to plant only a few high-yield varieties very intensively. What we lost in this transition were dozens of flavorful varieties that had been grown for generations in careful and sustainable farming practices built on the maintenance of rich soil structures that contributed the most flavor and nutrients to the grain grown in it.

When I wrote about my baking journey in the first bread book, I only briefly touched on one aspect that was in fact very central to the way I had come to approach making bread: using whole-grain and diverse types of grains to vary flavors and textures in a finished loaf. This aspect of baking was too big to properly address in *Tartine Bread*. It would demand its own book, and there was a lot more that I needed to learn and discover before presenting my take on whole-grain bread making.

This book chronicles my discoveries and experiences baking with whole grains for a dedicated slice of two years. Each bread here has its own unique story that tells of the people and places that inspired recipes and techniques. Many of the pastry recipes recall the days of our first bakeshop, when my wife and business partner, Liz Pruiett, and I began to express what we had learned abroad while embracing our adopted California idiom. Here we look to the past while pushing forward. It is, in some sense, a journey backward, an attempt to recapture the flavors of ancient grains, to rejoin our nascent age of invention. Yet many of the ways I use these grains are new—discovered well into the scope of this project and opening up unique and exciting possibilities for baking with flavorful grains. With the "old soul" intact, a quickening was in order.

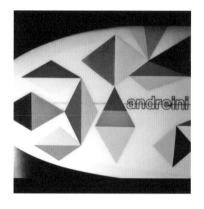

INTRODUCTION

WHOLE GRAIN PRIMER

The diverse grains we are exploring in this book can be generally divided into two groups: grains that have gluten quality and quantity sufficient to make bread with, and those that do not. Each grain has its own unique flavor and character; some are more distinct than others. All are well suited to bread and pastry making when the right techniques are employed.

The prevalent one-size-fits-all approach to baking—using generic wheat flours (white or whole wheat) and mostly white cane sugar—has severely restricted the range of flavors and textures in most commercially available baked goods.

Once you understand the different qualities, flavor and otherwise, that each grain brings to a recipe, you can blend different flours to get the flavor and texture you desire. The combinations are endless.

Here, we have settled on a range of bread and pastry recipes that illustrate the practical basics of use with results we like. Our final recipes and techniques are also determined by the overall aesthetic of the finished bread or pastry we are trying to achieve. In our bread, we are always after contrast: a tender, open crumb and substantial caramelized crust are the ideals, no matter what blend of flours we're using.

I'm using the term *grains* here in a general sense, as some of the ingredients we use as "grains" are not technically grains. Buckwheat, for example, is neither grain nor wheat but rather a pseudocereal from an herbal plant that is botanically related to rhubarb and sorrel. But because we treat all of the following ingredients as grains, we've chosen to keep it simple and call them that.

In some cases the grains are used whole—toasted, soaked and/or cooked, or sprouted before being mixed into the dough— to add distinct flavors and texture. When we use flours ground from the grains, we use freshly milled (if possible), either milled the same day or a few days prior. These recipes work with flours that are not freshly milled, although the flavor from freshly milled flour is different from flour that is a few weeks or months old, much the same way that the flavor of freshly ground black pepper differs from preground.

THE TARTINE METHOD

The varieties of wheat I find most exciting are the soft, high-protein wheats I was fortunate to discover and use in my recent European baking travels. These softer wheats can produce a more tender crumb and a loaf of bread that's easier to digest. The perception is that they are more difficult to work with because the delicate nature of the gluten makes the dough less tolerant of modern industrial production. But I've found the basic Tartine bread-making method especially well suited to making loaves with these types of wheats. The use of a low-acid, young natural leaven, gentle kneading, and a long slow rise preserves the strength of these softer wheats. Modern industrial ways of mixing bread doughs would be too rough for these flours.

In Denmark and Sweden, there has been a strong resurgence in both cultivating and using these softer wheats, many of them heirloom Scandinavian varieties that have been brought back into use through the decades-long work of baker-miller Jorn Ussing, who lives in the far north of Denmark and founded his iconic biodynamic bakery, Aurion, in Aalborg many years ago. To the same end, visionary farmer Per Grube, in partnership with Claus Meyer, has been working closely with grain research authority Dr. Anders Borgen, who founded Agrologica, a consulting firm in Jutland, Denmark, that collaborates with Per's farm and is dedicated to growing and reviving native grains. The grains are stone-milled into flour at a 250-year-old mill just over the border in Sweden. Last year, this locally grown fresh-milled flour was made available to Danish home bakers.

During my visits, I found dozens of varieties of Scandinavian wheats and ryes in use, along with new ones being cultivated and tested for flavor and baking qualities. Each subsequent visit I've made to Scandinavia, I've been able to experiment with grains that are new to me. In fact, this movement has seemed to be taking hold across the globe as I have found the same pattern in Germany, Austria, England, Ireland, Mexico, and Central and South America: a resurgence of more flavorful varieties of heirloom wheats brought back into cultivation, coupled with a search for how to make good bread using wheat that has such different qualities of gluten than the modern wheats that have been used for the last few generations. Thankfully, a parallel movement is happening in the United States, and many small-scale farmers are testing plots of heirloom wheat varietals to rediscover flavors that have not been tasted for generations. This revival mirrors the resurgence of heirloom fruits and vegetables and heritage breeds of poultry, pigs, and cows.

For me personally, working with this "new" collection of varied soft wheats is coming full circle. In the early part of my baking life, when I was helping open Dave Miller's bakery in Chico, California, in the early '90s, I worked with heirloom varietals of wheat grown by Fred Kirschenmann, a pioneering North Dakota farmer known for his work in sustainability and land ethics. Following that, I worked in France with Daniel Collin and Patrick LePort. Their favored grain was an obscure small spelt, or *petit epeautre* (technically einkorn), grown in the highest elevations of Provence. It was an exquisitely flavored, soft, ancient wheat that was very difficult to work with but, when coaxed by skilled hands into a loaf of bread, ultimately rewarding.

At the turn of the last century in many parts of the world, bread was often the heart of a meal. This was hearty bread, nourishing and flavorful, and meant to sustain a long day's hard work. Once I started on this book project, testing whole-grain varieties and blends with each bake, these became my preferred daily breads. During this period, a longtime bread customer stopped by on a day I was baking alone. The shop was closed—the bread I was baking was for a friend's holiday dinner event, but he was hoping to get a loaf. He asked what type I had baked. I told him I had made the basic Tartine country loaf. He asked what I'd be baking the following day, and I told him I had planned to make sprouted Kamut loaves. "I'll come back tomorrow," he replied. As he walked away, I realized that I would have done the same thing. We were open for business the next day and, inspired by his interest, I adjusted the recipe for our regular country loaf to incorporate a larger percentage of a whole-grain flour. Our customers shared my enthusiasm for the flavors of these whole-grain breads, which encouraged me to continue experimenting.

ABOUT THE BREADS IN THIS BOOK

All the breads in this book are made with blends of whole-grain, high-extraction, and sifted (much of the bran and germ removed) flours. *Extraction* is a measure of how much flour is extracted or milled from a given amount of wheat. The extraction rate is expressed as a percentage: If you start with 1 kilo of grain and end up with 700 grams of milled flour (30 percent of the coarse bran being sifted off), the extraction rate is 70 percent. Whole-wheat flour, in which the entire grain is milled and the bran and germ are left in the flour, is 100 percent extraction. As such it should be labeled "100 percent stone-ground whole-grain flour," but this is not always the case; for this reason it's helpful to know how the miller supplying your flour mills and labels.

Commercially available white (sifted) bread flour has an extraction rate of 70 to 75 percent, and is made up mostly of the starchy endosperm, with the bran and germ having been removed. When I call for high-extraction flour, as I do in many of the recipes in this book, I'm calling for flour that has an extraction percentage around 85 percent, somewhere between white flour and whole-wheat flour, with a portion of the coarse bran sifted off. Most of the recipes, including our country dough that we first made in Point Reyes Station, also call for adding raw wheat germ, which adds flavor and nutrition.

Because we are using a higher percentage of whole grain, the hydration (amount of liquid absorbed by the flour) is higher than typical breads made with mostly white flour because the fiber particles contained in whole grains absorb much more water than sifted white flour absorbs. In the master method recipes in this book we start at 85 percent hydration, which results in a very wet dough; porridge breads have a lower base hydration because the porridge further hydrates the flour. If you're feeling nervous about working with such a wet dough, reduce the hydration to 80 percent and you'll have no trouble—the dough will be drier and easier to work with. At Tartine, for these breads we typically use hydration percentages in the low to mid-'90s.

Another major consideration when making bread with whole-grain flours is the length of the *autolyse*, or rest period after the flour and water are combined. The autolyse is always important when making bread, but

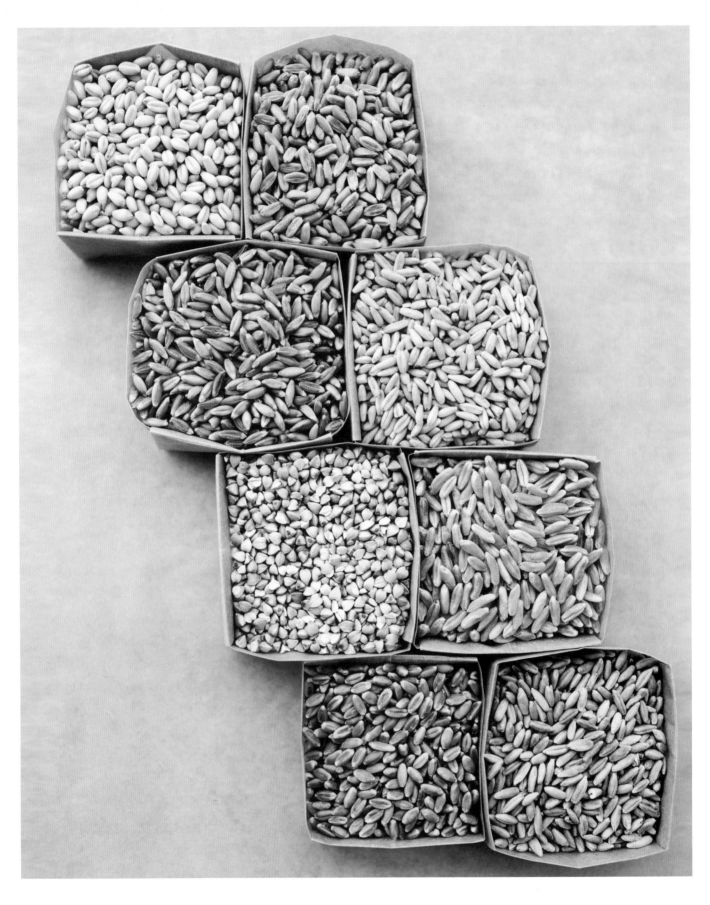

because of the higher liquid absorption of whole grains, these breads will benefit from a longer autolyse. All recipes in this book call for a minimum 30-minute autolyse, but 2 to 4 hours or even overnight will yield even sweeter tasting bread. As the autolyse is increased, *amylase* (enzymes in the dough that break down complex sugars), which is activated by the water, starts to release sugars in the flour, making them more available for the wild yeasts and bacteria when the natural leaven is introduced to the dough. Some slightly bitter grains such as red wheat take on a noticeably sweeter tone with a longer autolyse. All the doughs are more active once the leaven is incorporated, and their crusts will caramelize to a deeper golden hue due to the increase of available sugars.

THE FRENCH LOAF

In France, after World War II, breads made with whole-grain dark rye and buckwheat that had been eaten during wartime were quickly replaced with whiter breads. The preference for baguettes and other lighter styles of bread spread from Paris to rural areas, where country people wanted to eat city bread. (The rustic country-style miche became something of a relic, until it was revived a generation later by Lionel Poilâne in Paris, when the city folks wanted to eat country bread.)

During the war, millers added bean flour and other less savory fillers to make up for the lack of available wheat. Later, the French government enacted strict regulations to control the quality of flour and account for exactly how much of the bran and germ had been removed; the whiter the flour, the higher the price. At that time, France arguably still made the world's finest bread, and rustic country loaves were not traded out for Wonder bread as they were in the United States. The farmer and miller were driving quality and diversity in the evolution of French bread to meet the demands of the bakers, who wanted to distinguish themselves from the competition. Milling became a very specialized endeavor, with no less than half a dozen different extractions available, each containing more or less of the whole grain, along with many more custom blends. The trade was elevated to a vaunted craft and science. Coupled with the traditional use of natural leaven, these different varieties of sifted flour were pioneered and put into commercial use to make exquisite loaves during what has been called the golden age of French bread.

The limited collection of white and whole-wheat flours grew into a diverse family of breads, their qualities determined by the extraction percentage and blend of the milled grain. *Campagne* was the country bread made with medium-extraction flour, often with a small portion of rye flour added. *Complet* was mostly made of higher extraction flour that contained more whole grain but with much of the coarse bran sifted off. *Integral* loaves were made with the highest extraction flour: close to or completely whole grain. These breads are still made today and are more popular than ever.

HOW TO MAKE HIGH-EXTRACTION WHEAT FLOUR

To make the high-extraction flour at home that I call for in this book, start with freshly milled or store-bought whole-grain flour and pass it through a fine-mesh sifter. You'll capture some of the bran in the sifter, thereby "extracting" it from the flour. Save the bran to coat the outside of your loaves to prevent them from sticking to the cloth lining the basket over the long rise. Or save it to use in recipes that call for bran.

Because the screen method can be somewhat variable, dependent on how coarsely the grain is milled and how much bran is captured in the screen, you can also use this alternative method to make high-extraction flour: Blend 100 percent whole-grain flour with white (sifted) flour in the ratio of 50 percent whole-grain flour to 50 percent white flour.

ABOUT MEDIUM-STRONG WHEAT FLOUR

When I call for medium-strong wheat flour in this book, I mean "bread" flour, or a blend of bread and all-purpose flours. Ideally, for blending with many of the softer wheats used in these recipes, I am looking for a flour that has 11 to 12 percent gluten with good

baking qualities to add strength to the dough while avoiding the toughness and difficult digestion added by generally flavorless high-gluten flours.

A Note About the Baker's Percentages and Metric Measurements

Note that all the bread recipes in the book give measurements for ingredients in both baker's percentages and grams. Using metric measurements is by far the most precise way to measure ingredients for bread and pastry baking. If you don't already own a digital scale, I highly recommend you purchase one; it's essential for the bread recipes in this book, and helpful for the pastry recipes, too.

When a recipe is written in baker's percentages—typically used for bread recipes in the profession—all ingredients are expressed by weight by ratio, and in percentages relative to the flour, which is always 100 percent. As in my previous book, I don't include the flour that is in the natural leaven in the 100-percent flour weight. The same is true for poolish, the prefermented batter used in combination with leaven for some breads, such as baguettes. At Tartine, we always have leaven on hand at different stages and use it in many different types of recipes, so I treat leaven as an ingredient component in the percentages. It is much simpler this way, especially when baking at home or in small batches at restaurants.

EMMER, SPELT, AND EINKORN

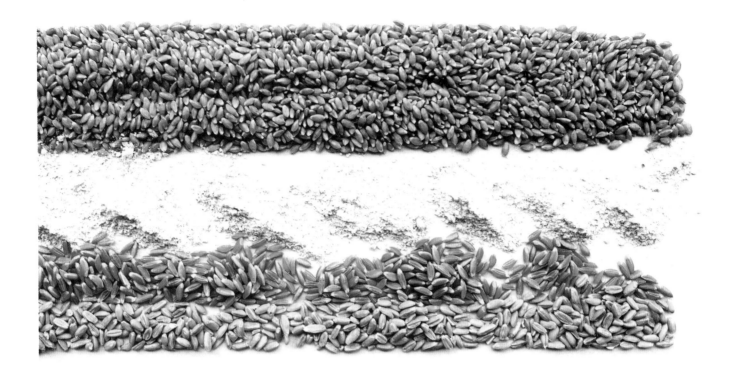

These ancient wheats have rich flavors, more delicate gluten, and higher protein than common wheats, making them easier to digest, especially when fermented with a natural leaven. They are more difficult to harvest and process using modern farming methods, and thus have fallen out of general production for generations. As interest grows in the rediscovered range of flavors, my hope is that they will again become more widely available. For now, you can find them at natural foods stores and online.

Emmer (*Triticum dicoccum*) is an ancient hard durum wheat still commonly used to make pasta in Italy, where it is also called *farro*. Emmer has a more delicate gluten and is higher in protein than common wheat.

The copper-colored **spelt** (*Triticum spelta*) grain is one of the more popular and easy-to-find heirloom varieties of wheat. Called *dinkel* in Germany and

Austria, where it is still used extensively to make breads, spelt is thought to be a natural hybrid of emmer. The gluten structure in spelt, as well as other heirloom wheats, differs from that of modern common wheat in that it's much more extensible and much less elastic. It's a softer type of wheat with a bit less tolerance of super-hydration and very long rising times (the acid breaks this gluten down quickly), character traits that make them all easier to digest. Spelt is also higher in protein and vitamins than common wheat.

Einkorn (*Triticum monococcum*), which literally means "single grain," is the oldest cultivated wheat, ancestor to all others. Tasting both grassy and nutty, this is another grain with delicate gluten. Einkorn is perhaps the most difficult of these ancient wheats to find and, because of the small amount of this exceptional grain grown, it can be quite expensive. Thankfully this trend seems to be reversing.

KAMUT AND SEMOLINA

Kamut (also called **Khorasan**) is a large, golden-colored hard durum wheat that is grown in parts of Egypt, Turkey, and Italy. Kamut International is a company in Montana that has trademarked the grain and name Kamut; it grows this delicious grain across the plains of Montana and North Dakota. Kamut is a sort of wonder grain, and can be used to make both bread and pastry. It's 20 to 40 percent higher in protein than modern wheats.

Semolina is golden-yellow flour made from the endosperm of modern durum wheat. Although it's more commonly used to make pasta than bread (except in Sicily, where semolina bread is traditional), I love the sweet grain flavor that it adds to bread, and sometimes use it together with its ancient relative, Kamut.

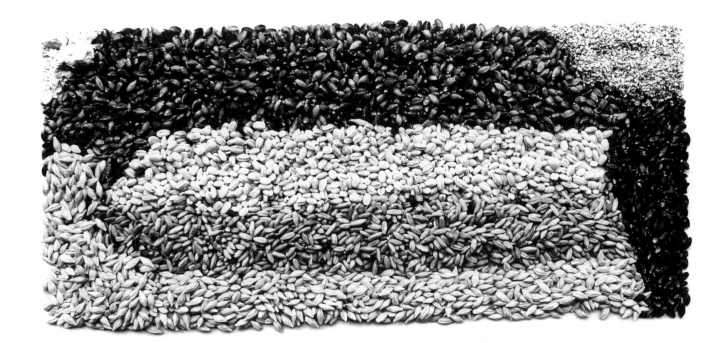

Rye is a blue-gray-green-colored grain used to make traditional Eastern and Northern European breads. It is very low in gluten and high in a curiously strong vegetable gum that makes it simultaneously slick, sticky, and able to bind water. Rye has a distinctive, tangy flavor; the unusual character of rye benefits from using natural leaven in the sourdough tradition, which helps to favorably condition the dough. Rye can also be used in pastry recipes to add a different flavor profile to cookies, tea cakes, pastry shells, and tart crusts. All of the rye flour we use is whole-grain dark rye, not the refined "white" rye flour that is also available.

Barley is a light cream–colored grain that is very high in fiber and low in gluten. It is believed to be the oldest cultivated grain in the world. Sprouted or cooked into a porridge before being added to bread dough, barley adds a subtle, earthy flavor to breads. Barley is well suited for use in pastry as well.

Buckwheat is a pseudocereal from a plant closely related to rhubarb. It has a strong flavor, and the whole-grain flour has a very dark (almost black) color. Buckwheat has no gluten. We use it to add flavor to breads, but only utilizing new techniques that bend the math in the flour-to-hydration ratio, such as cooking the groats into a porridge or double-fermenting the grains before adding them to dough. Buckwheat adds no structure and using too high of a percentage as a portion of the flour weakens the dough. In certain pastry doughs in which gluten development is less of a concern, using some or all buckwheat flour creates quite a distinct flavor and color.

Cracked corn (the store-bought version is sold as "coarse grits" or "polenta") adds a sweet flavor and golden color, along with a glistening viscosity, to breads when it is cooked into a porridge before it is added to the dough. Using heirloom red and blue cracked corn porridge yields different corn flavors and colors. We use finer ground cornmeal to add this distinct flavor and color to pastries and toasted, sweet cornmeal to flavor baguettes.

Oats are high in protein, fat (compared to other grains), and fiber and have no gluten. We use cooked or prefermented oats in bread, blended with stronger grains, and oat flour in pastries to add wholesome richness and tender body to tea cakes and cookies.

BROWN RICE, MILLET, AMARANTH, QUINOA

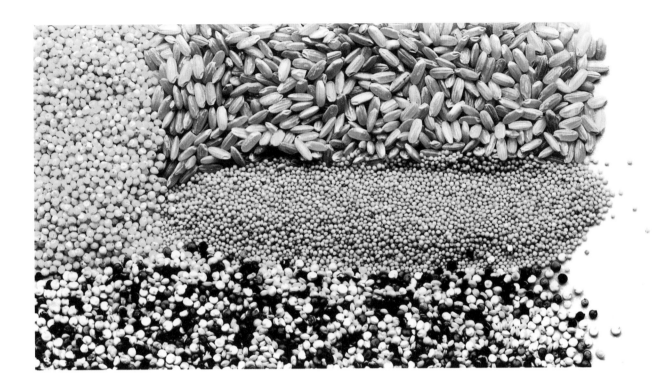

Brown rice is simply the whole-grain rice kernel with all of the nutritious and flavorful bran, germ, and oils left intact. When brown rice is processed into white rice, a moderate portion of the protein as well as 50 to 80 percent of the nutrients are lost, leaving primarily starch behind.

Growing up in the late '70s and early '80s, when my mom had our house on a pseudomacrobiotic diet part of the time, I came to love brown rice and couldn't really understand why anyone would favor bland (in comparison) white rice to its more satisfying whole-food equivalent.

Millet, a small cereal from seeded grass, has been eaten for thousands of years as a staple food in Africa and Asia, and contains no gluten.

Amaranth and quinoa are both pseudograin seeds that once comprised a large part of the native Mexican and Central and South American diet and figured prominently in Aztec, Mayan, and Incan religious practices. Both are valued for their nutritive qualities: Quinoa has 60 percent more protein than wheat and barley, and amaranth, while close to matching quinoa's protein levels, is higher in lysine (an essential amino acid) than any other grain. Both are exceptionally good nutrient complements when combined with other grains to make lush whole-grain breads. We use them cooked, as a porridge addition, or sprouted to flavor hearth loaves. The plants are closely related to spinach and chard, and indeed lend a pleasantly nutty chardlike flavor to bread. Both amaranth and quinoa have no gluten.

WHOLE GRAIN PRIMER

MASTER METHOD FOR TARTINE LOAVES

One of my bakers at Tartine had tried for over a year to get a job working with us on the bread shift. At the time, he was managing another bakery in the area and making great bread, but in a style that was different from ours. Every couple of months, he'd bring me a loaf of bread he had made and leave a note asking if we had any openings for a position on our team. The bread he left for me was always quite good, but at a certain point, he left a loaf that was indistinguishable from my own. As soon as I had a shift open up, I called him in. The last bread he left was impressive: it had all the qualities we aim for in a Tartine loaf. And that was exactly the point—after tasting our bread for the first time, he decided that's what he wanted to focus on mastering as a bread baker. I remembered the very same thing had happened to me after tasting Bourdon's bread so many years ago. Our bread had the qualities that he loved as well, and now— it was as much his bread as ours.

Tartine bread is built within a system that defines our approach to baking. Based as much on means as on ends, Tartine bread must possess a handful of specific qualities that have defined my ideal since the beginning. The doughs must be made with the best-quality organic, biodynamic, freshly milled grains with ample hydration, slow and gentle mixing, and long rising time using a natural leaven. The basic country loaf method is straightforward, based on the French *levain* tradition with a few key deviations. Through extensive experimentation over the last few years, we've found many new ways to reach that ideal. The basic method, with emphasis placed on these Tartine peculiars, follows. Once you understand the method well in practice, it will give you a solid foundation from which to venture into new territory, exploring our modern approach using diverse whole grains.

MASTER METHOD FOR TARTINE LOAVES

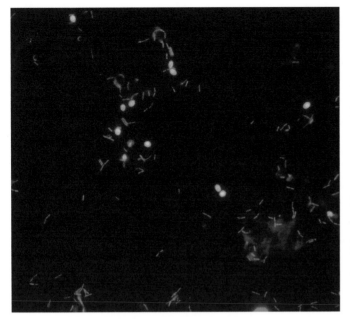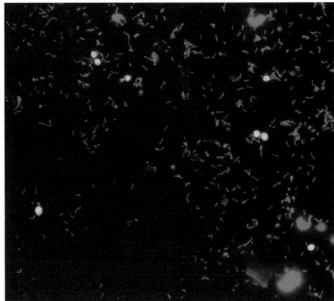

Tartine natural leaven: wild yeast and lactobacteria

Make the 50/50 Flour Blend: Mix 1250 grams of bread flour— all-purpose flour will work as well—half white and half whole-wheat. You will use this 50/50 Flour Blend to feed your culture and develop your starter.

Make the starter: In a medium bowl, place 300 grams of slightly warm (80 to 85°F/26 to 29°C) water. Add 315 grams of flour blend (reserve the remaining flour blend), and mix with your hand or a wooden spoon to combine until the mixture is free of any dry bits. Cover the mixture with a clean, dry kitchen towel or cheesecloth and let stand at warm room temperature until bubbles start to form around the sides and on the surface, about 2 days. It's important to maintain a warm temperature. Let stand another day to allow fermentation to progress a bit. More bubbles should form. This is your starter. It will smell acidic and slightly funky. At this stage it's time to train your starter into a leaven by feeding it fresh flour and water at regular intervals.

Feed the starter: Transfer 75 grams of the starter to a clean bowl and discard the remainder of the starter. To the 75 grams of starter, add 150 grams of the 50/50 Flour Blend and 150 grams warm (80 to 85°F/26 to 29°C) water. Mix to combine; it should have the consistency of pancake batter. Repeat this feeding process once every 24 hours at the same time of day, always transferring 75 grams of the starter to a clean bowl and discarding the remainder, then adding the flour and water and re-covering the bowl with a clean, dry kitchen towel after each feeding and letting the mixture stand at warm room temperature. The batter should start to rise and fall consistently throughout the day after a few days of feedings. As the starter develops, the smell will change from ripe and sour to sweet and pleasantly fermented, like yogurt. Once this sweet lactic character is established and the fermentation (the regular rise and fall of the batter) is predictable, a few days to one week, it's time to make the leaven from this mature starter.

Matured starter

Leaven readiness test

Make the leaven: The leaven is the portion of prefermented flour and water that will go into your final dough and raise the whole mass during the bulk (first) and final rises. Two days before you want to make bread, feed the matured starter twice daily, once in the morning and once in the evening (the process described on the facing page) to increase fermentation activity. When you are ready to make the dough, discard all but 1 tablespoon of the matured starter. To the remaining 1 tablespoon, add 200 grams of the 50/50 Flour Blend and 200 grams warm (80 to 85°F/26 to 29°C) water. This is your leaven. Cover and let rest at moderate room temperature for 4 to 6 hours.

To test the leaven's readiness, drop a spoonful into a bowl of room temperature water. If it sinks, it is not ready and needs more time to ripen. When it floats on the surface or close to it, it's ready to use to make the dough.

To maintain the leaven for regular use, continue feeding daily as described at left. To save leaven for long periods without use, add enough flour to make a dry paste and keep covered in the refrigerator. When you want to use it again, keep at warm room temperature for at least 2 days and do three to four feedings to refresh and reduce the acid load that builds up while it is stored in the refrigerator.

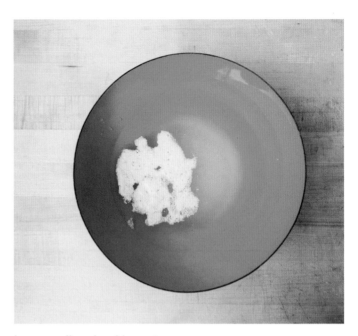

Leaven dissolved in water

Make the dough/premix: In a large mixing bowl, combine the flours called for in each recipe. If the recipe calls for wheat germ, add the germ to the flour now. In a second, large mixing bowl, add all but 50 grams of the liquids specified in the recipe. Add the amount of leaven specified in the recipe to the liquids and stir to disperse. Add the flour to the liquid-leaven mixture and stir to combine until no dry bits remain. For porridge breads, stir in the cooked and cooled porridge until incorporated.

Premix

Final mix

For the autolyse: Cover and let the premix rest for at least 30 minutes and up to 4 hours (or overnight for doughs made with hard wheat flours) to hydrate during this rest period, taking care to keep the mixture where it is at warm room temperature.

For the final mix: After autolyse, add the salt specified in each recipe and the remaining 50 grams of slightly warm water, folding the dough on top of itself to incorporate.

Bulk rise

Folding and turning

For the bulk rise: Transfer the dough to a medium bowl and keep covered to maintain a warm dough temperature of 80 to 85°F/26 to 29°C to accomplish the first rising time, 3 to 4 hours. Wet doughs benefit from a warmer bulk rise, gaining more strength and structure from the very active fermentation. Alternatively, you can accomplish the same goal more slowly by fermenting the dough overnight at cellar temperature (55°F/13°C).

To fold and turn: During the bulk rise, the dough is developed by folding and turning it in the container. Fold the dough every 30 minutes for the first 2½ hours of bulk rising. To do a fold, dip one hand in water, grab the underside of the dough, stretch it out, and fold it back over itself. Rotate the container one-quarter turn and repeat three to four times. When you are folding the dough, note its temperature to the touch and how the dough is becoming aerated and elastic. When adding dry, presoaked seeds, porridge, sprouted grains, or cracked grains to the dough, fold them in after the first two series of turns, about 1 hour into the bulk rise. After 3 hours and six foldings, the dough should feel aerated, billowy, and softer. You will see a 20 to 30 percent increase in volume. If not, continue bulk rising for 30 minutes to 1 hour longer.

After bulk fermentation

Divide and shape

To divide and shape: When the dough is 20 to 30 percent increased in volume, billowy, and elastic, remove it from the container with a dough spatula. We don't "punch" the dough down to de-gas at Tartine. We strengthen the dough by using gentle folds and turns. As flavor develops during the first rising, it is key to preserve that flavorful gas built up within the dough until the bread is baked. Lightly flour the top surface of the dough and cut into two pieces using the dough spatula. Work each piece gently into a round by drawing the spatula around the side of the dough in a circular motion. Surface tension builds as the dough anchors to the surface while you rotate and work it. Again, take care to work the dough gently to preserve the flavorful gasses that have formed during fermentation. When well shaped, the dough should have a taut, smooth surface.

For the bench rest: Lightly flour the tops of the rounds, cover with a kitchen towel, and let rest on the work surface for 20 to 30 minutes. Line two medium baskets or bowls with clean, dry kitchen towels and dust generously with a 50/50 mixture of any wheat and rice flours. Starchy rice flour (whether white or brown) is more absorbent than wheat flour and keeps the dough from sticking to the cloth-lined rising basket. Tapioca flour can also be used.

MASTER METHOD FOR TARTINE LOAVES

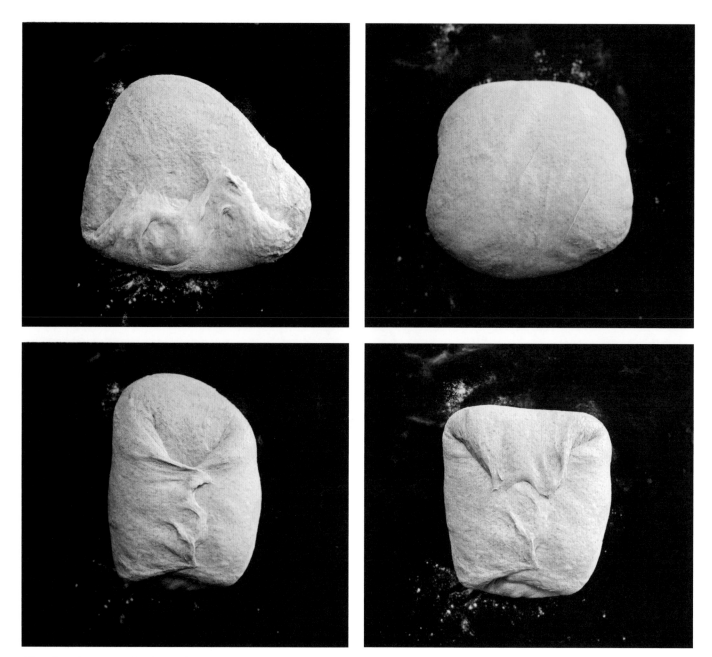

Shaping (counterclockwise)

For the final shaping: Slip the dough spatula under each piece of dough and flip it, floured-side down. Pull the bottom of the dough up to fold into one-third of the round. Pull each side and fold over the center to elongate the dough vertically. Fold the top down to the center and then fold the bottom up over the top fold-down, leaving the seam underneath. Let the dough rest for a few minutes, seam-side down, so that the seam seals.

Final rise, seam-side down

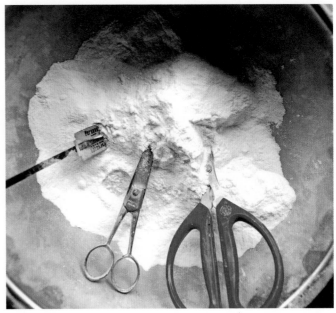
Scoring tools

For the final rising: Transfer the dough to the floured baskets, flipping the dough over so that the seam side is facing up and centered. If the recipe calls for the loaf to be coated in seeds or cracked or flaked grain, roll the smooth side of the dough in the coating before transferring it to the floured rising baskets, placing the dough coated-side down, seam-side up. Cover with a clean, dry kitchen towel and let rise at warm room temperature for 3 to 5 hours or overnight in the refrigerator.

To bake: Twenty minutes before you are ready to bake the bread, preheat the oven to 500°F/260°C, adjust the oven rack to its lowest position, and place a 9½-in/24-cm round cast-iron Dutch oven, 11-in/28-cm oval cast-iron Dutch oven, or any other heavy ovenproof pot with a tight-fitting lid into the oven to preheat (with its lid on).

Carefully transfer one dough round into the preheated Dutch oven, tipping it out of the basket into the pot so it is now seam-side down.

Score the top of the dough with a razor blade or cut with scissors. Cover the pot and return to the oven. After 20 minutes, reduce the oven temperature to 450°F/230°C. Bake another 10 minutes, then carefully remove the lid (a cloud of steam will be released). Continue to bake for another 20 to 25 minutes, until the crust is a deep golden brown.

When it's done, turn the baked loaf out onto a wire rack to cool. To bake the second loaf, raise the oven temperature to 500°F/260°C, wipe out the Dutch oven with a dry kitchen towel, and reheat with the lid on for 15 minutes. Repeat the baking procedure as with the first loaf.

MASTER METHOD FOR TARTINE LOAVES

BASIC BREADS

We are in the midst of an exciting time, which manifests as a modern movement promoting identity-preserved grains and other heirloom vegetables, and giving chefs, bakers, and home cooks a much wider range of flavors to work with. Thinking more from a chef's perspective than that of a traditional bread baker, I find myself drawn to the artistry of blending and layering flavors and less to the dogma of using only one variety of a grain to make my bread, just as wine makers ferment different grapes together to make compelling wines, or baristas combine coffee beans to achieve espresso with complementary distinctions of flavor in a single pull. Our expanding scope of identity-preserved cultivars elegantly fills out the bigger picture of overall biodiversity; the crux, I propose, is how we use them.

My approach to using whole-grain flours in bread baking is mostly a complete departure from the traditional tack of swapping out white flour for whole-wheat flour, but I do start simply here in this chapter. This first section of basic breads introduces a few formulas in which different types of flours are blended to give specific flavor characteristics while carefully tailoring the nature of crust and crumb. Some flours used here have very little or no gluten but strong flavors, so they are used in small quantities to layer their personality into the disposition of the bread. Our basic Tartine country loaf is made up of at least five different flours with percentages that we adjust throughout the year to maintain consistency in the finished loaves (despite variances in the flours, water, and climate) or to shift the bread's temperament in new directions. The ingredients, of course, are not the sole factor in determining the character of the final loaf, but starting with only three components—flour, water, and salt—makes choosing them carefully a huge part of the equation. This chapter is the foundation for the new approach to baking with these flours and a short warm-up for the swift move to new techniques that build progressively throughout the book.

WHITE-WHEAT BLEND (ODE TO BOURDON)

Hard red wheat, the most common variety used for bread flour, often has a slightly tannic, bitter flavor. This is one reason that so many whole-grain breads have sweeteners added. When I was fresh out of culinary school I apprenticed with Richard Bourdon, a classically trained concert musician–turned-baker, who had settled in the Berkshires in western Massachusetts. It was Bourdon who introduced me to naturally leavened bread, and I learned a great deal from him. At the time, Richard had six young children, and he was committed to making a whole-grain sandwich bread kids would love. Blending red wheat with a less tannic white-wheat variety reduced this bitterness, making the dough naturally "sweeter." To this day, when making whole-grain breads, I prefer the sweeter flavor gained by using a blend of wheats, as I find that the tannin of straight hard red wheat overpowers other subtle flavors developed during the long rise. An optional overnight autolyse further helps counter the bitterness.

FLOUR	BAKER'S %	WEIGHT
High-extraction wheat flour	50	500 g
Whole-grain wheat flour	25	250 g
White whole-wheat flour	25	250 g
WHEAT GERM	7	70 g
WATER	85	850 g
LEAVEN	15	150 g
FINE SEA SALT	2.5	25 g

Follow the master method on pages 34 to 37 to make the dough. Then, follow the instructions for rising, shaping, and baking on pages 38 to 41.

Yield: Two loaves

WHEAT-RYE 10%

With little gluten to speak of—nowhere near enough to properly bind a loaf of bread as wheat does—a bread made from rye relies heavily on pentosan vegetable gum to give it body and a structure of sorts. Rye, along with buckwheat, is one of the few grains used to make bread that has a flavor notably distinct from the family of wheats. When rye is fermented with natural leaven it develops a certain sour flavor that lovers of Scandinavian and German breads cherish. In the recipes presented here, small amounts of rye flour are used both to flavor and change the texture of the finished loaf. In this "slight rye" loaf, containing 10 percent rye flour, the rye flavor is faint but perceptible; the gum adds a glistening sheen and tenderness to the crumb.

FLOUR	BAKER'S %	WEIGHT
High-extraction wheat flour	40	400 g
Medium-strong bread flour	40	400 g
Whole-grain dark rye flour	10	100 g
Whole-grain wheat flour	10	100 g
WHEAT GERM	7	70 g
WATER	85	850 g
LEAVEN	15	150 g
FINE SEA SALT	2.5	25 g

+ RYE FLAKES FOR COATING (OPTIONAL)

Follow the master method on pages 34 to 37 to make the dough. Then, follow the instructions for rising, shaping, and baking on pages 38 to 41.

Roll the shaped dough in rye flakes to coat. Place in the baskets, flake-side down seam-side up, for the final rise.

Yield: Two loaves

WHEAT-RYE 20%

When you start using 20 percent or more rye flour in bread dough, the character of the grain becomes more pronounced. As the rye percentage increases, the crumb becomes more dense and cakelike, and the sour flavor more assertive. To preserve an open crumb using higher percentages of rye flour, I developed different techniques, including fermenting rye berries before adding them to bread dough (see page 171).

FLOUR	BAKER'S %	WEIGHT
High-extraction wheat flour	40	400 g
Medium-strong bread flour	30	300 g
Whole-grain dark rye flour	20	200 g
Whole-grain wheat flour	10	100 g
WHEAT GERM	7	70 g
WATER	85	850 g
LEAVEN	15	150 g
FINE SEA SALT	2.5	25 g

Follow the master method on pages 34 to 37 to make the dough. Then, follow the instructions for rising, shaping, and baking on pages 38 to 41.

Yield: Two loaves

BASIC BREADS

BUCKWHEAT WITH TOASTED GROATS & CRÈME FRAÎCHE

Buckwheat has always been a favorite grain and lends a haunting, earthy flavor to many of the world's great cuisines, whether sarrasin crêpes of Brittany, delicate soba noodles from Japan, pasta and polenta in the Italian Alps, or hearty soups and stews across Central and Eastern Europe. When I first traveled to Hungary with my friend Nick Balla, chef at Bar Tartine, the bakery's sister restaurant, we feasted on crimson-colored Mangalitsa pork sausage on bread, topped with spiced lardo and shaved onions. The sausage was outstanding; the bread, not so much—it was bleached white and puffed up with little flavor.

Mangalitsa pork is renowned for its exceptionally creamy and flavorful fat. At home, a farmer friend was raising Mangalitsa pigs for us to use at Bar Tartine, and Nick, inspired by our trip, was curing lardo and making his own paprika sausages. I wanted to create a bread that would complement these bold flavors. Gluten-free buckwheat contributes even less structure to a dough than rye, but its flavor is equally distinct. To work enough buckwheat to taste into this dough without weakening it, we added toasted buckwheat groats as you would add nuts or seeds. To create a loaf with an open crumb using even higher percentages of buckwheat, I developed different techniques (as seen here and the recipes on pages 132 and 150).

FLOUR	BAKER'S %	WEIGHT
High-extraction wheat flour	50	500 g
Medium-strong wheat flour	45	450 g
Whole-grain buckwheat flour	5	50 g
WHEAT GERM	7	70 g
WATER	85	850 g
LEAVEN	15	150 g
FINE SEA SALT	2.5	25 g

ADDITIONS

	BAKER'S %	WEIGHT
Buckwheat groats, toasted (see page 190), soaked in warm water to cover for 1 hour, then drained	15	150 g
Crème fraîche	7	70 g

+ COARSELY GROUND BUCKWHEAT GROATS FOR COATING (OPTIONAL)

Follow the master method on pages 34 to 37 to make the dough.

In a medium bowl, combine the groats and crème fraîche. After the first two series of turns,

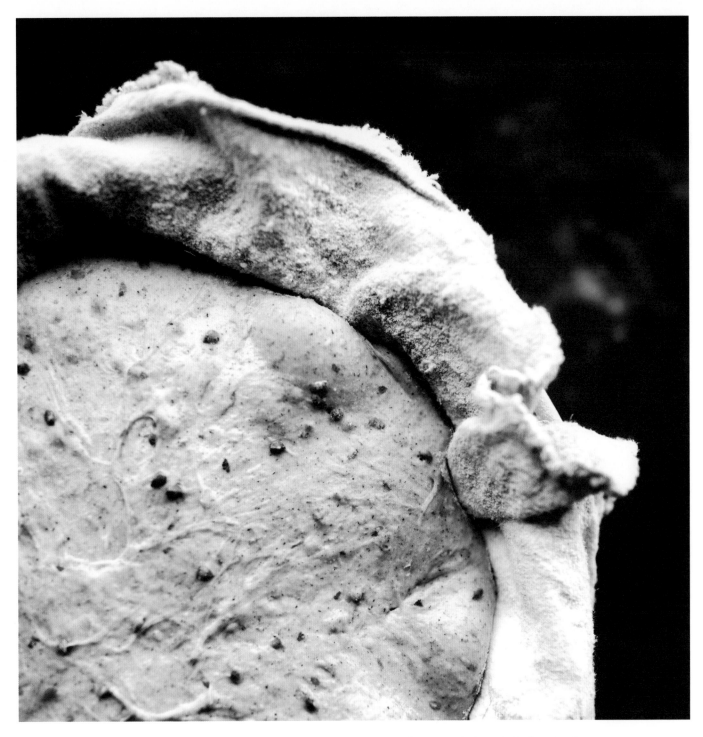

about 1 hour into the bulk fermentation, add the groats mixture gently by hand until incorporated into the dough. Then, follow the instructions for rising, shaping, and baking on pages 38 to 41.

Roll the shaped dough in buckwheat groats to coat. Place in the baskets, groat-side down, seam-side up, for the final rise.

Yield: Two loaves

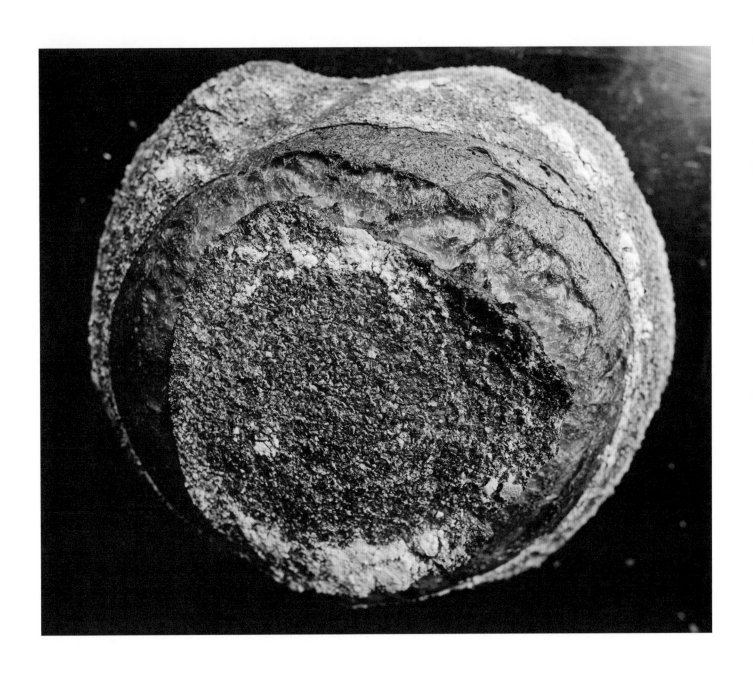

BASIC BREADS

MASTER METHOD FOR POOLISH

Poolish, as employed at Tartine, is a pre-fermented batter made up of roughly equal parts by weight of flour and water (or milk for some enriched doughs) with a very small amount of commercial yeast added. Poolish is typically prepared a few hours to up to a full day ahead of when it will be used in the dough. Poolish that has fermented overnight will have more time to develop flavor than the 3- to 4-hour preparation, but younger poolish typically has more leavening power. Certain recipes, like the Tartine baguette, call for a combination of both overnight (about 12 hours) and same-day (3 to 4hours) poolish to deliver the qualities of both. The long, slow fermentation for many hours before use allows a sweet, yeasty flavor to develop that will enrich the final dough. Poolish also conditions the dough in certain ways, increasing extensibility and enabling one to achieve a lighter texture and thin, crisp crust, which is what I'm after in breads like baguettes, flatbreads, and brioche.

I always use poolish in combination with natural leaven. While the improvements in flavor and dough conditioning are evident when using a poolish, using natural leaven in combination will always yield a more flavorful loaf that keeps better.

125 g warm water (78°F/26°C)
⅛ t active dry yeast
125 g all-purpose or other specified flour

For same-day poolish: In a medium bowl, combine the water and yeast, then gradually add the flour, mixing with a wooden spoon until a smooth batter forms. Let stand for 3 to 4 hours at warm room temperature (75 to 80°F/23 to 27°C).

For overnight poolish: Let the mixture stand (covered) overnight in the refrigerator.

SPELT & TOASTED CORN-FLOUR BAGUETTES

At Tartine, baguettes are discussed in expectant tones; we talk about what we hope to achieve. Inspiration comes from unexpected directions, and the model isn't always so clear at the outset. Keeping a sharp, open mind is the key to discovery.

This recipe for spelt baguettes revealed itself in the form of a char-blistered flatbread, my version of Persian barbari bread that I made for my chef friend Samin Nosrat. Cooking alongside her mother, Samin prepared a traditional Persian feast as part of her Afterhours series which are held once a month at the bakery. My contribution to Samin's generous gatherings is always a special bread that is baked just as everyone is being seated for dinner. This was a flatbread made with multiple preferments and baked on two different decks in the oven to simulate a sort of tandoori effect. I realized that the flatbread was getting closer to the true flavor I was looking for in our baguette.

My first Tartine baguette recipe, published in *Tartine Bread*, has an aroma of freshly popped corn when properly made. This is an aroma I had detected in some of my favorite baguettes in Paris, both at Maison Kayser and at Boulangerie du Pain et des Idées. In fact, many of

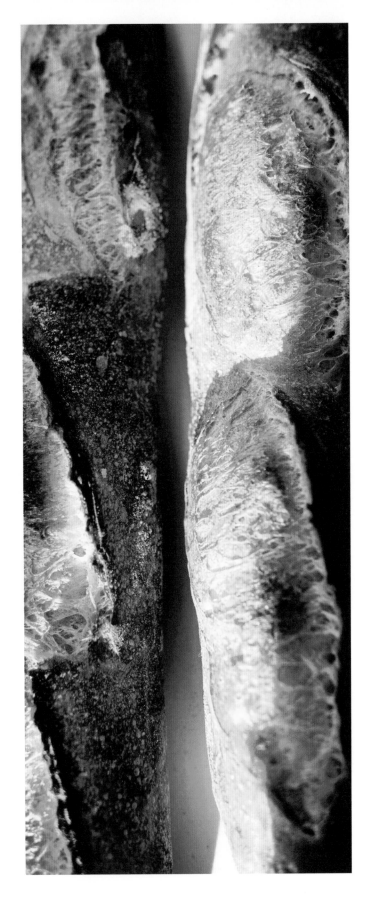

the breads I sampled from both bakeries had an inexplicable toasted corn aroma and sweet flavor that was as delicious as it was unexpected. Sweet corn is a flavor Americans know well, but it's not readily associated with artisan French bread.

While searching for an explanation, I learned that this sweet corn flavor was in vogue at the time in Paris and millers were, at the request of bakers, adding a small amount of very carefully toasted sweet-corn flour to the flour mix, which added a tasty natural sweetness and enticing aroma to the resulting bread. It is a flavor the Parisians were mad for and, notably, one that the French have little reference for, since corn is not indigenous to Europe; this fresh new flavor was captivating to them.

This new baguette recipe is a hybrid of my flatbread experiments, utilizing more whole grain and a small amount of corn flour. Using high-extraction spelt flour in the dough and higher percentages of preferment and natural leaven produces a baguette with more overall depth of flavor, in contrast to so many baguettes available today. One of the preferments is made with emmer, which adds its own subtle sweetness. The ideal crumb should be lacelike, pearlescent, and very tender, while the crust should be thin, crisp, and pleasantly toasty. To achieve this, the dough is made from a blend of very soft flours that together push the limits of contrast in crust and crumb—the resulting baguette stands apart.

	BAKER'S %	WEIGHT
Overnight poolish (see page 58)	25	250 g
Same-day poolish (see page 58)	25	250 g
WATER	55	550 g
LEAVEN	50	500 g
Yeast	0.2	2 g
FLOUR		
Medium-strong bread flour	50	500 g
High-extraction spelt flour	30	300 g
All-purpose flour	20	200 g
Raw wheat germ	7	70 g
Toasted corn flour	4	40 g
FINE SEA SALT	3	30 g

The overnight poolish should be prepared a day ahead, using white sifted bread flour. The same-day poolish is prepared the morning of the day the baguettes will be made, using half emmer flour and half spelt flour. Let the same-day poolish stand, covered, for 3 to 4 hours at warm room temperature (75 to 80°F/ 23 to 27°C) before mixing the baguette dough.

To mix the baguette dough, put the water and leaven into a large mixing bowl. Add the overnight and the same-day poolishes and the yeast and stir to disperse. Add the bread flour, spelt flour, all-purpose flour, wheat germ, and toasted corn flour and, using your hands, mix thoroughly until no bits of dry flour remain. The baguette dough initially will feel a bit stiff but it will soften during bulk fermentation. Let the dough rest, covered with a kitchen towel, for 25 to 40 minutes, then add the salt and mix gently by hand to combine.

Transfer the dough to a clear container, cover, and begin the bulk fermentation at a temperature of about 75°F/23°C (see page 38) for about 3 hours. Fold the dough every 30 minutes as instructed on page 38.

When the bulk fermentation is complete, divide the dough into four or five pieces (approximately 400 grams each) depending on the size of your baking stone. Shape each piece into a rectangle with rounded corners. Let rest on the work surface, covered with a kitchen towel, for 30 minutes.

Drape a large kitchen towel over a baking sheet or cutting board and dust with rice flour.

Shaping baguette dough is difficult because much more handling is required than for other shapes. With practice and persistence, it will become second nature. Working with one rectangle of dough at a time, fold the third of the dough closest to you up and over the middle

third. Holding the ends of the dough, stretch it horizontally so that it doubles in width. Fold the third of the dough farthest from you over the middle of the elongated rectangle as if closing the flap of an envelope. Press on this flap to develop tension in the dough. Using your palms and fingers together, roll the dough toward you; with each successive roll, press with the outer edge of your palms and fingers to further develop tension in the dough. Set the dough on the work surface. Place both palms on top of the dough cylinder and roll it back and forth, stretching the dough to elongate the shape and taper the ends, while keeping in mind the length of your baking stone.

Place the loaves on the floured towel seam-side up, separating them with folds in the towel. Bring the sides of the towel over the loaves on each end to support the outer edges. Let rise at room temperature (70 to 75°F/21 to 26°C) for 1½ hours, then transfer to the refrigerator, covered, to chill for another 1½ to 2 hours. The cooler and shorter rising time is due to the use of faster-acting commercial yeast in the recipe.

Place the baking stone on the middle rack of the oven and preheat the oven to 500°F/260°C. When using a baking stone, the trick is to saturate the oven with steam when you start baking. The best way to get as much steam as possible into a home oven is to place a baking sheet lined with water-soaked kitchen towels in the bottom of the oven as it is preheating. As the oven heats, the moisture in the towels produces steam. Ideally, you want the oven to be steaming for 15 minutes after you load the baguettes to bake. Take care to get the baguettes into the oven quickly and shut the door; the more steam that stays in the oven during the first part of baking, the better the oven spring, or volume, of the finished loaves. The steam will also help develop a thin, crisp crust with a slight sheen.

Using rice flour, dust a pizza peel and dust the seam side of the baguettes. Holding the towel, flip each loaf onto a hand peel and then slide it onto the pizza peel. Depending on the size of your oven and baking stone, you may have to bake the baguettes in batches; keep the remaining loaves in the refrigerator until you're ready to bake them. Place the loaves side by side on the peel about 2 in/5 cm apart. With a double-edged razor (to ensure less drag), score each loaf down the center with a series of slightly overlapping lines. Make sure your oven is fully saturated with steam; you'll notice steam escaping from openings around the oven door. Open the oven door, slide the baguettes onto the baking stone, and quickly shut the door to retain as much steam as possible. Immediately reduce the oven temperature to 475°F/240°C.

Once the baguettes start to color, after 15 minutes, carefully remove the pan holding the kitchen towels, which should be dry. Continue to bake the loaves until they are a deep golden color, 10 to 15 minutes more. Serve warm from the oven or let cool on a rack.

Yield: Four to five baguettes

ANCIENT GRAINS

Kamut is an ancient durum wheat that was introduced to me by Dave Miller when Liz and I traveled from the Berkshires to California to work with him in 1993. Dave was an early adopter, one of the first bakers using the group of wheats that were collectively referred to by grain geeks like me as "ancient grains," including Kamut and the spelts. He was also using pseudocereal grains that were relatively unknown at the time, like teff and amaranth, to flavor his breads. Almost all of Dave's wheat was grown by the now-legendary farmer Fred Kirschenmann in North Dakota, and was the first grown in the United States to be certified biodynamic by the Demeter Association.

Dave had worked years before with Richard Bourdon and was back for a visit at a time when I was ready to move on and continue learning from a baker with different techniques. I was used to working with "wet" doughs from my training with Bourdon, but Dave, using mostly whole grain for all of his breads, pushed the hydration levels even higher and actually used water on the work surface instead of flour when shaping his loaves. Dave's method was radical and unorthodox; he also milled his own flour and advocated using freshly milled grains. I had lots to learn.

For an intense year, it was just the two of us making bread. Most of what I learned from Dave was unspoken. The best passive teaching is not quick, but it goes deep. Liz was tasked with applying classic technique to create pastries using whole grains and unrefined sugars, making discoveries along the way that would inform our modern approach to using these ingredients years later.

After working with Dave, Liz and I traveled to France to begin our apprenticeships with Daniel Collin and Patrick LePort. Patrick was also using Kamut, as well as a precious heirloom French small spelt (einkorn), *petit épeautre*, that is grown only in the high altitudes of Provence.

Kamut, spelt, einkorn, and emmer form the core group of these heirloom variety wheats (there are many more varieties). All are high in protein and contain sufficient gluten to make bread. But the character of the gluten is more delicate than common wheats and, when fermented with a natural leaven over a long rise, ensures that these breads are typically easier to digest than breads made with common wheats.

ANCIENT GRAINS

KAMUT 60%

Compared to red wheats, Kamut has a flavor I think of as naturally sweet and, when Kamut is used as a high percentage of the flour for the dough, it gives the loaf a light golden color. Due to the high protein in Kamut flour, this dough can take a lot of water. At Tartine, we typically push the hydration up beyond 90 percent, which helps create the lacy, open crumb we work to achieve.

FLOUR	BAKER'S %	WEIGHT
Whole-grain Kamut flour	60	600 g
Medium-strong wheat flour, sifted	20	200 g
High-extraction wheat flour	20	200 g
WHEAT GERM	7	70 g
WATER	85	850 g
LEAVEN	15	150 g
FINE SEA SALT	2.5	25 g

+ KAMUT FLAKES FOR COATING (OPTIONAL)

Follow the master method on pages 34 to 37 to make the dough. Then, follow the instructions for rising, shaping, and baking on pages 38 to 41.

Roll the shaped dough in Kamut flakes to coat. Place in the baskets, flake-side down seam-side up, for the final rise.

Yield: Two loaves

ANCIENT GRAINS

ANCIENT GRAINS

EMMER/EINKORN

The ancient flavor of emmer and einkorn—nutty and grassy—is much more pronounced than that of modern wheat. The French *petit épeautre* I first encountered while baking in Provence twenty years ago is an einkorn; I've had a taste for the grain since. While the protein content of these grains is high, the gluten quality is not well suited to achieving strong dough if used in high percentages (60 percent or more) with ample hydration. But using only 30 percent whole-grain emmer or einkorn flour blended with slightly stronger (higher protein) flours yields a loaf with the aesthetic qualities I aim for, coupled with the distinct flavor of the grain.

FLOUR	BAKER'S %	WEIGHT
Medium-strong wheat flour	40	400 g
Whole-grain emmer or einkorn flour	30	300 g
High-extraction wheat flour	30	300 g
WHEAT GERM	7	70 g
WATER	85	850 g
LEAVEN	15	150 g
FINE SEA SALT	2.5	25 g

+ COARSE BRAN FOR COATING (OPTIONAL)

Follow the master method on pages 34 to 37 to make the dough. Then, follow the instructions for rising, shaping, and baking on pages 38 to 41.

Roll the shaped dough in coarse bran to coat. Place in the baskets, bran-side down seam-side up, for the final rise.

Yield: Two loaves

ANCIENT GRAINS

SPELT-WHEAT

Ancient spelt wheat is comparable to the modern wheats we use today in many applications. While this soft, high-protein grain has a nutty flavor, it also has a fair measure of strength and extreme extensibility and is especially useful for adding certain characteristics to bread doughs, such as an exceptionally tender and open crumb. Here I've blended whole spelt with high-extraction spelt, plus two modern wheat flours to add the elasticity needed to create a Tartine loaf.

FLOUR	BAKER'S %	WEIGHT
High-extraction spelt flour	30	300 g
Medium-strong wheat flour	30	300 g
High-extraction wheat flour	30	300 g
Whole-grain spelt flour	10	100 g
WHEAT GERM	7	70 g
WATER	85	850 g
LEAVEN	15	150 g
FINE SEA SALT	2.5	25 g

+ SPELT FLAKES FOR COATING (OPTIONAL)

Follow the master method on pages 34 to 37 to make the dough. Then, follow the instructions for rising, shaping, and baking on pages 38 to 41.

Roll the shaped dough in spelt flakes to coat. Place in the baskets, flake-side down seam-side up, for the final rise.

Yield: Two loaves

DENMARK

My introduction to the breads of Denmark took place on the coast of Northern California. I'd tried the blue-black Danish whole-grain rye bread called *rugbrød* after we opened our wood-fired bakeshop in Point Reyes. Some of the first friends we made after landing in California from France were Michael and Marianne Weiner and their daughters Sara and Karen. We spent holidays at their generous gatherings and they adopted us into their community, a rich one that

at the ideal temperature for baking this style of bread, Marianne proposed a trade: She would bring her rye breads over and load them into my oven when I was done baking for the day, and in exchange for the oven space, she'd help me get my bread bagged and delivered around town. It was a trade that worked well for six years, until we both moved with our families from the country to San Francisco. I've been selling Marianne's rye bread in our shop at Tartine Bakery since we opened in 2002; these

View near Ystad

included Alan Scott, who built our first wood-fired oven and gave us a place to live straightaway.

At the time, I was baking a few hundred loaves a day in a very hot wood-fired oven. All the bread was baked at over 575°F/300°C, but the oven never had a chance to cool below 400°F/200°C. Sure, we cooked most nights in the oven, and had lots of great dinner parties, but there was a load of potential heat energy wasted at that lower temperature when I wasn't baking. I was already working sixteen-plus-hour days, and the small bakeshop was connected to our house, so I wasn't keen on renting it out to another baker.

Marianne had been making her mother's recipe for traditional Danish rugbrød and had periodically considered making it for commercial sale. Noticing my empty oven sitting vacant

Kille making crispbreads

days, she delivers her baked bread to me.

Many years later, Liz and I set off to take our young daughter Archer to an intensive physical therapy camp in a small Polish fishing village on the Baltic Sea. Studying maps while planning our travels, we noted that the Polish village is directly across from Scandinavia, and not far at that. Clearly, it was time to finally visit Denmark, to taste rugbrød in its native habitat. I looked up an old friend, Danish chef Kille Enna. She and I had met when she was in Northern California doing research for her cookbook Cuisine of the Sun, and had stayed in touch since. I asked if she could direct me to anyone there making interesting breads with native Scandinavian grains, and she set me up to explore the regional breads of Denmark. So Liz, Archer, and I arrived in Berlin via London, bread starter in tow. We rented a car and headed northeast

Greenhouse at Fuglebjerggaard

In large part due to Meyer's work, the Nordic region, particularly Denmark and Sweden, was at the forefront of a progressive culinary movement defined by wild whole foods, much of it foraged, and the fusion of modern and traditional cooking techniques. A key part of this ongoing exploration is the restoration of Scandinavian heirloom grains. For two decades, Meyer, with the help of dedicated farmers, grain researchers, millers, and bakers, has been working to reintroduce these grains into the food culture. What they are beginning to achieve was a revelation to me.

I also had the opportunity to taste the Danish *rugbrød*. It is eaten in thin slices topped with infinite combinations of cured meats, vegetables, smoked fish, and more to comprise a daytime meal or snack generally referred to as *smørrebrød*, which literally translates as "butter bread." Refreshingly, white flour and white breads aren't typical of the region. I enjoyed the excellent breads, but what

Tomato jam

Christian Puglisi at Bar Tartine

toward Poland. After settling my family into the camp and reviving my bread starter, I made my way to Copenhagen.

Kille met me there and we set out to make bread at Hemmingstrupvej, Camilla Plum's farm just outside of the city. Plum is an authority on Scandinavian food traditions and Per Kølster, her partner at the time, was growing Nordic wheats and ryes, as well as hops, which were being used to make the beer served at Noma restaurant. Plum stone-mills the grains daily to make her exceptional breads.

Although it was late January, the height of winter, her greenhouses were filled with thousands of varieties of plant starts for the coming growing season. I later learned that her farm is home to one of the largest organic seed banks in northern Europe (outside of Svalbard Global Seed Vault in Norway, which is not exclusively organic).

On my first visit baking with Plum at her farm, we used a Nordic wheat called

Dragon. According to her, this was the only place on the planet growing this strain of wheat at that time. They preferred the flavor of Dragon to that of Öland, the wheat in vogue during this time that year and used at Noma, Relae, and select bakeshops to make a distinctly delicious bread. Öland wheat is a purely Nordic variety, named for the island it was originally grown on in Sweden; its flavor and aroma are exceptional.

After spending a few days baking on the farm, we returned to Copenhagen, where Enna introduced me to Claus Meyer, the Danish chef-baker and self-described gastro-entrepreneur, founder of the Meyer Group. Meyer kickstarted the progressive Nordic food movement, having opened Noma in 2003 with visionary chef René Redzepi and founded the Nordic Food Lab, a think tank dedicated to stretching the region's culinary possibilities.

really impressed me was the variety of grains—dozens of heirloom Nordic wheats and ryes—that the bakers had at their disposal and that I'd never before seen used in the States.

Meyer, sensing my enthusiasm, graciously opened his bakeshops to me, and I was invited to make bread using the Nordic grains. He suggested I teach a class at his cooking school, the Meyers Madhus, on making bread using stone-ground Nordic wheat. The only problem was, I had never worked with Nordic whole-grain flours before, so I had no idea what the outcome would be. Plus there was no bread oven at the Meyers Madhus; I'd have to bake the bread in heavy iron pots—the method detailed

Frost on red chard

in *Tartine Bread*. Meanwhile, bakers, farmers, and millers from across Denmark and Sweden signed up for the class. Claus also invited journalists from television stations, Denmark's two largest newspapers, and food magazines.

and again at his more casual sister restaurant, Manfred's. Christian's food is incredibly focused, at once simple yet complex, and completely transcends any type of regional description. The food I ate there haunts me still: I remember the taste of every dish.

Christian invited me into Relae's kitchen to see how they made their house loaves. I already had so much respect for this team and the way they operated and was excited and honored to talk bread with them. At Meyer's Bakery, across the street from Relae, I had been using freshly stone-milled Nordic wheat, mixing the dough pretty much as I would at home using the natural leaven I brought from San Francisco and had been maintaining with the native flour.

The bread turned out far better than any of us had expected. The Danish bakers were astonished that a loaf made with a large portion of whole grain with natural leaven could

Coffee with Camilla

Sensing my concern, Nicolai Skytte, who at that time was the chief baker in charge of Meyer's bakeries, invited me to do some test baking. It was nice to know that someone was watching out for me, given how far I was from home. It was around this time that I started to notice that the

Scandinavians were more open to new ideas and flavors, as well as sharing their own, than any other place I'd lived or worked. They were both interested and interesting, freely sharing recipes and techniques. In the world of competitive and highly secretive chef's kitchens, this creative sort of open sourcing was refreshing.

The bakery Nicolai was running then is located on a street called Jægersborggade in the Nørrebro neighborhood. Home to young artists and artisans along with a large population of North African immigrants, it's more dynamic and diverse than much of the

have such a light texture and achieve such volume. They had even apologized in advance for the quality of the flour, saying it had been a bad year for wheat in Denmark. In spite of this, the bread turned out as good, or better, than anything I'd made back home, proof that we were working with very high-quality grain.

The bread demo at Meyers Madhus was a complete success, thanks to Nicolai and the Meyers team, and owing much to the excellent Nordic grains. Denmark was, and remains, in the midst of a bread revolution, and the accidental timing of my visit could not have been better. It was there that I began to recognize the possibility and promise of a more diverse family of whole-grain varieties. I left Denmark inspired to experiment.

Ølandshvedebrod ay Meyers Bageri

rest of the pristine city. My weeks spent baking on this block reminded me of San Francisco's Mission District, where Tartine is located. Across the street from the bakery is the renowned Coffee Collective (at which we thankfully had a tab) and a progressive restaurant called Relae run by a singularly inspired chef, Christian Puglisi, who would become a good friend. Christian was a key sous chef during the early years at Noma before going on to open Relae.

Christian was making delicious bread at Relae, an elemental country-style loaf similar to my own, based on a natural leaven and made using the Nordic wheat varieties. During the week leading up to my class, I had dinner twice at Christian's places: once at Relae

SEEDED BREADS

When adding ingredients to breads, I keep it simple, with the aim always first to complement the flavor of the grain. Mostly I'm making breads that will be eaten with other foods, so this is also a consideration. I want to make sure the bread can complement a meal. And because I want to taste the flavor of the grain, I'm careful not to overload the loaf with competing flavors.

SUNFLOWER-FLAXSEED

This is another variation of an old favorite recipe. Soaked flax and sunflower seeds lend a glistening sheen to the crumb of this hearty take on one of our classics, with an added percentage of whole-wheat flour blended with high-extraction flours and fresh wheat germ.

FLOUR	BAKER'S %	WEIGHT
High-extraction wheat flour	50	500 g
Medium-strong wheat flour, sifted	30	300 g
Whole-wheat flour	20	200 g
WHEAT GERM	7	70 g
WATER	85	850 g
LEAVEN	15	150 g
FINE SEA SALT	2.5	25 g

ADDITIONS

Flaxseeds	14	140 g
Hot water	18	180 g
Sunflower seeds, lightly toasted	14	140 g

+ RAW SUNFLOWER AND FLAXSEEDS FOR COATING (OPTIONAL)

Follow the master method on pages 34 to 37 to make the dough.

In a medium bowl, combine the flaxseeds and hot water and stir together. Let cool, then add the sunflower seeds, stirring to incorporate.

After the first two series of turns, about 1 hour into the bulk rise, add the presoaked seed mixture gently by hand until incorporated into the dough.

Then, follow the instructions for rising, shaping, and baking on pages 38 to 41.

Roll the shaped dough in raw sunflower and flaxseeds to coat. Place in baskets seed-side down seam-side up, for the final rise period.

Yield: Two loaves

SEEDED BREADS

SEEDED WHEAT

Poppy, toasted sesame, caraway, and sunflower seeds layer dense and savory flavors over the sunflower-flaxseed base. Additional delicious seed combinations are legion.

FLOUR	BAKER'S %	WEIGHT
High-extraction wheat flour	50	500 g
Medium-strong wheat flour	30	300 g
Whole-grain wheat flour	20	200 g
WHEAT GERM	7	70 g
WATER	85	850 g
LEAVEN	15	150 g
FINE SEA SALT	2.5	25 g

ADDITIONS		
Flaxseeds	10	100 g
Hot water	18	180 g
Unhulled sesame seeds, toasted	10	100 g
Poppy seeds	10	100 g
Sunflower seeds	5	50 g
Pumpkin seeds	5	50 g
Caraway seeds, toasted and ground	5	50 g

+ RAW FLAX, SESAME, POPPY, AND CARAWAY SEEDS FOR COATING (OPTIONAL)

Follow the master method on pages 34 to 37 to make the dough.

In a medium bowl, combine the flaxseeds and hot water and stir to combine. Let stand until cool, then stir in the sesame seeds, poppy seeds, sunflower seeds, pumpkin seeds, and caraway seeds.

After the first two series of turns, about 1 hour into the bulk rise, add the presoaked seed mixture gently by hand until incorporated into the dough.

Then, follow the instructions for rising, shaping, and baking on pages 38 to 41.

Roll the shaped dough in a mixture of raw seeds to coat. Place in the baskets seed-side down seam-side up, for the final rise.

Yield: Two loaves

SEEDED BREADS

SEEDED BREADS

SESAME-WHEAT

Across the board, chefs love the umami flavor of toasted sesame seeds, and I am no exception. The first bread I tasted at Richard Bourdon's Berkshire Mountain Bakery was his sesame-wheat bread. I'm often asked why I decided to become a baker; for many years I had no rational answer. Writing this now, I can honestly say that it was Bourdon's sesame bread that did it. Liz and I brought some of Bourdon's bread home and I made grilled cheese sandwiches with slabs of Comté cheese, fried in plenty of olive oil in a cast-iron skillet. Twenty years later, I am still making the same sandwich at home at least once a week.

My chef friend Mathias Dahlgren invited me to make bread to celebrate the fifth anniversary of his iconic restaurants in the Grand Hôtel Stockholm. To honor the occasion, I made this bread with remarkable Swedish flour, stone-milled for us the day before at Warbro Kvarn Mill, a few hours northeast of the city, where the biodynamic heirloom wheat was grown.

FLOUR	BAKER'S %	WEIGHT
High-extraction wheat flour	50	500 g
Medium-strong wheat flour	30	300 g
Whole-grain wheat flour	20	200 g
WHEAT GERM	7	70 g
WATER	85	850 g
LEAVEN	15	150 g
FINE SEA SALT	2.5	25 g

ADDITIONS		
Unhulled sesame seeds, toasted	25	250 g

+ RAW SESAME SEEDS FOR COATING (OPTIONAL)

Follow the master method on pages 34 to 37 to make the dough.

After the first two series of turns, about 1 hour into the bulk rise, add the toasted sesame seeds gently by hand until incorporated into the dough.

Then, follow the instructions for rising, shaping, and baking on pages 38 to 41.

Roll the shaped dough in raw sesame seeds to coat. Place in baskets seed-side down seam-side up, for the final rise.

Yield: Two loaves

SEEDED BREADS

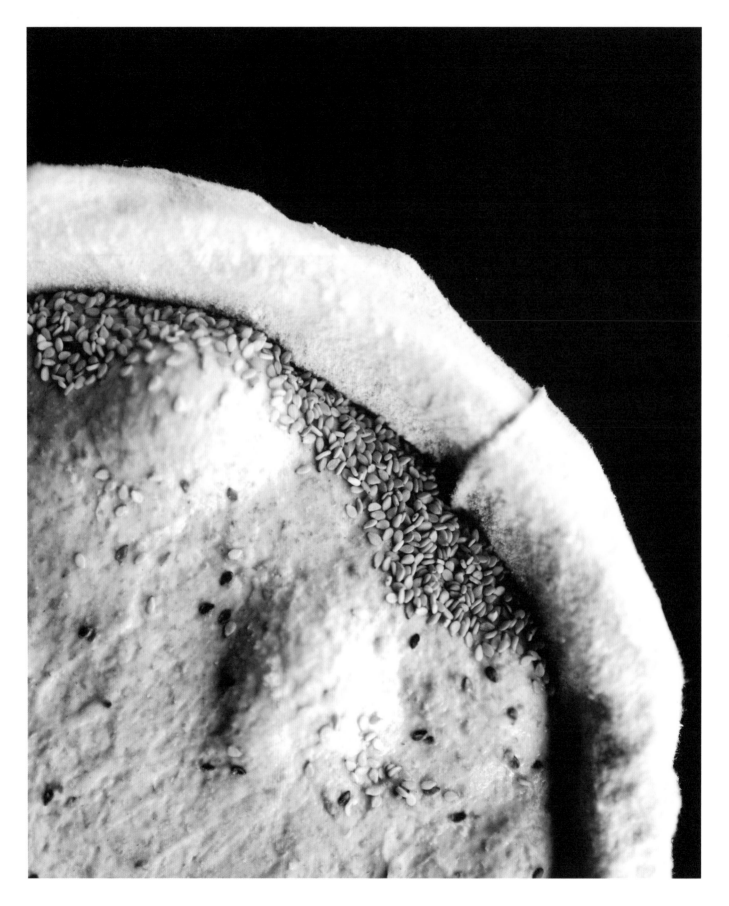

SEEDED BREADS

WHEAT-RYE CARAWAY-CORIANDER

This is a Tartine sort of landbrot, an Alpine-style country bread, inspired by my time spent working with bakers in the mountains of Austria during the annual wood-fired-oven bread festival in late summer. Made with a portion of whole-grain rye, whole-wheat, and high-extraction flours, this bread is flavored with a traditional combination of toasted crushed caraway and coriander seeds.

FLOUR	BAKER'S %	WEIGHT
Medium-strong wheat flour	45	450 g
High-extraction wheat flour	25	250 g
Whole-grain wheat flour	20	200 g
Whole-grain dark rye flour	10	100 g
WHEAT GERM	7	70 g
WATER	85	850 g
LEAVEN	15	150 g
FINE SEA SALT	2.5	25 g

ADDITIONS

Caraway seeds, toasted and coarsely ground	2	20 g
Whole coriander seeds, toasted and coarsely ground	2	20 g

+ RYE FLAKES FOR COATING (OPTIONAL)

Follow the master method on pages 34 to 37 to make the dough.

After the first two series of turns, about 1 hour into the bulk rise, add the caraway and coriander seeds gently by hand until incorporated into the dough.

Then, follow the instructions for rising, shaping, and baking on pages 38 to 41.

Roll the shaped dough in rye flakes to coat. Place in baskets flake-side down seam-side up, for the final rise.

Yield: Two loaves

SEEDED BREADS

SWEDEN

It was my friend Ignacio Mattos, a chef in New York City, who first mentioned Stockholm to me. He had been cooking a distinctly rustic style of Italian food for years at the first Il Buco on Bond Street in New York when he met Swedish chefs Mathias Dahlgren and Magnus Ek. They sensed a kinship in Ignacio's approach to cooking and invited him to visit Sweden. On a recent trip to Paris, Ignacio had experienced a bold new creative direction on the restaurant scene that was lighting up the city and he was eager to explore what chefs were doing in Scandinavia. After much planning, Ignacio was set to visit Stockholm with Mathias and his chef-partner Martin as guides. Mathias, lover of bread, butter, and cured pork fat to spread on it, is a national treasure. Father of the elegant and modern natural style of Scandinavian cooking, he

Copenhagen with dinner at Noma. Ignacio returned to the States refreshed, with a sort of desperate inspiration that would inform his next restaurant in New York.

Ignacio's project in New York was a restaurant named Isa, in Williamsburg, Brooklyn, just over the bridge from Manhattan. He had originally imagined it as a place serving locally sourced rustic food, the menu shaped by a central wood-fired oven and grill. But after his travels he switched gears, delving deep into a heady study of "modern primitive" cuisine that was largely informed by his travels. It was clearly the right path: The restaurant earned a James Beard Award nomination for Best New Restaurant less than four months after opening, an unprecedented nod to the leading-edge work that Ignacio and his kitchen were pioneering in the shadow of Manhattan.

Bon Appétit magazine went on to name Isa and its founding chef and owner on its list of international tastemakers of 2012.

Isa was as polarizing as it was visionary, and it didn't last long in this rare form. But the fearless spirit of exploration was transformative. There was no going back for any of us now; it was clear that this challenging journey would be rewarding in ways that might take years to realize.

Ignacio's stories fueled my own curiosity. I liked his true-believer tone—the trip had forced him to reevaluate his cooking—he was going someplace new with what he had learned. To understand what he had experienced, I would have to visit Sweden myself. It was clear to me that my close friend had been changed by his travels, that

Norrström River, Stockholm

brought home the coveted Bocuse d'Or prize in 1997.

What followed for Ignacio was a whirlwind tour of Stockholm and Copenhagen that began at the restaurants of Mathias Dahlgren, where he observed an extraordinary camaraderie among professionals, all pushing the envelope, exploring new flavors and working on ideas informed by ancient culinary traditions. He journeyed on to Magnus Ek's exquisite Oaxen Krog, an inn and restaurant with lush gardens on the island of Oaxen in the Swedish archipelago, an hour from Stockholm, and then to Mistral in Stockholm, the very personal vision of Fredrik Andersson, dedicated to an extreme sort of natural cuisine. The theme continued in

what he had seen had rewired his style of cooking. I wanted to go there, too. If Paris was the catalyst for his changed philosophy, Scandinavia was the quickening.

I had already planned to be in Copenhagen for the release of Tartine Bread; Ignacio easily convinced me to add a quick detour to Stockholm. A friend told me about a mythical wood-fired bakery on the island of Gotland called Rute Stenugnsbageri where they were making wet doughs with a higher percentage of hydration and natural leaven using native grains. I found a website for the bakery, and the images of the bread looked like a whole-grain version of bread I would have made on a good day at Tartine.

I sent a query to Martin Berg, and he wrote back with great news. His wife worked as one of the chief garden designers at Rosendals Trädgård, the royal botanical gardens of Stockholm. On the grounds of the garden seasonal bakery and had just closed for the start of the winter. I would have to save my visit there for another trip, but I learned that the founding baker of Rosendals, Tina Fernlund, a Scandinavian baking legend, was one half of the baking team operating the bakery on Gotland, working together with another Swedish baking icon, Erik Olofson. The Scandinavian bread world was getting smaller.

Like Denmark, Sweden is another country that prizes its golden yellow butter and dark rye bread and I was quickly settled upon arrival in Stockholm. The first evening of my visit found me generously fed by Mathias at his Food Bar, and the next morning Martin delivered me to a lovely day's work at Rosendals. The following day, Martin took me to meet Stefan Berg, the young head baker at Valhalla bakery, who supplies bread—really good bread—to Mathias's restaurants. Stefan is passionate and proud of his work. He is also

Grand Hôtel Stockholm

a master of many traditional Swedish classics, including my favorites, the *kardemummabullar*—cardamom buns. I liked both Stefan's bread and his attitude, and wanted to spend more time learning from him, but my trip was coming to a close. So when he mentioned a desire to visit California for a dose of inspiration and an opportunity to work at Tartine, I could not believe my good fortune. I agreed to host him under one condition: that he teach us to make the cardamom buns and his delicious crispbreads.

At the end of my first visit, on the drive to the airport, Martin asked if I would return to Sweden. Mathias and the whole staff would be celebrating the restaurant's fifth anniversary at the Grand Hotel Stockholm in a few months' time, and Martin asked if I was interested in making the bread for the celebration. I was beyond honored by the invitation.

With Bo Bech, Tina Fernlund, Mathias Dahlgren, Martin Berg

Gingerbread houses, Valhalla Bageriet

there was also a renowned wood-fired oven bakeshop, the only one in Stockholm, where they were baking with biodynamic Swedish grains. He had arranged for me to spend a day or two there working alongside the bakers. Martin himself spent three years baking at Rosendals off and on before settling in the savory side of the kitchen as a chef, which explained his extensive knowledge and interest in bread. At the time I visited, the bakeshop was fully staffed by women bakers, something I was used to from the early years at Tartine. I spent a wonderful day working with them that felt much like being at home.

Unfortunately, Gotland was not so quick and easy to get to from Stockholm, and would have added considerable travel time to my tight schedule. Plus, my baking companions at Rosendals informed me that Rute Stenugnsbageri was a

A few months later I returned to Stockholm and took the Arland Express to the heart of the city. Joining this company of friends, the warm welcome reminded me of Ignacio's description from his first visit. I arrived in Mathias's kitchen and was greeted

with bags of biodynamic Swedish grains that had been freshly stone-milled a day before at Warbrokvarn, a small mill a couple of hours northeast of Stockholm near Martin's country cottage. One bag contained sprouted, flaked spelt, and it seemed a good idea to soak the grains overnight in the whey they had just strained off of the house-made yogurt before adding them to the dough. It was the first time that I'd tried this method: basically prefermenting the grain that I would later incorporate into the dough as a flavoring agent, a way of adding more whole-grain flavor to a loaf without sacrificing the open texture and crust of the finished loaf.

I was devising recipes and scaling various ingredients in Mathias's basement kitchen in preparation for the dinner when Bo walked straight up and gave me a hug. Bo stands over 6 feet/2 meters tall— it was a bona fide bear hug, accompanied by his big smile. Within the hour, I was introduced

to another chef collaborator, Tina Fernlund, who was making a traditional Swedish dessert for the meal. Turns out we had all been trying to cross paths; we talked about bread for hours that afternoon while Bo and Tina prepped, and I set my bread doughs to rise overnight.

Another friend, Carol Choi, who was working at the time in the Fäviken kitchen north of Stockholm, rode the train down to help me with the bread, and the next couple of days were a wonderful celebration of good food produced by skilled hands working together.

After our bread duties were finished, Martin arranged for me to visit the Warbro Kvarn mill, where the grains I was using during the week had been grown and milled. Tina offered to

Orchard at Rosendal's garden

I was charged with making the bread for the meal; Mathias had invited a couple of other chef friends to contribute courses to the celebration. One of them was Bo Bech, a distinctly original and celebrated Danish chef from Copenhagen. I had just missed meeting him at his restaurant the day before, and was pleased to see him in Stockholm. Bo and Mathias had been friends for years; I had heard lots about Bech's outsized character and had been trying to meet him for some time. Bo had founded a legendary, if short-lived eponymous bakeshop with a signature bread, the only bread offered, that proved as elusive as the man himself. On my previous trips to Copenhagen I had barely missed Bo and his bread (always sold out) a couple of times, finally making it to his shop a few days after it closed for good; he'd sold it to Claus Meyer. Bo's bread shop is now Meyer's Bakery on the King's Road where I had baked bread to mark the release of my first book a few days before.

drive, and I was thrilled to spend the day with a fellow baker who had long inspired me from afar. The countryside in Sweden was lush and green; we arrived at Warbro Kvarn and were met with tasty fresh breads and cakes baked by the miller and his family. All of the biodynamic heirloom grains were grown on the land surrounding the mill. The fresh-milled flours and sprouted grain products that were produced by this small family operation were some of the finest grains I've ever worked with.

On the drive back to the city, I felt a tinge of fretfulness amidst the bounty of inspiration. The flavor of the grain I was able to work with both in Copenhagen and Stockholm was better than anything I had ever worked with at home. The striking dedication, skill, and creative support I found in the kitchen of Mathias and Martin set the bar impossibly high. As I left this new family to rejoin my own, a mountain loomed large in my mind. I had more work to do, and it was time to start climbing.

Stefan's bread at Valhalla

HEARTH LOAVES WITH SPROUTED GRAINS

Sprouting grains is a way to make them edible and more digestible without cooking. Sprouting—technically germination—is the point when the seed begins to transform from a grain into a plant through an enzymatic process that breaks the starch molecules into simple sugars to fuel plant growth. Inherent nutrients, vitamins, and minerals stored to nourish the plant typically increase at germination, and are rendered more accessible and easy to absorb for us. When we eat sprouts at this point, we are digesting them more as a vegetable rather than a grain.

When I finally made my way to Denmark to begin researching Scandinavian breads, I was constantly advised not to eat too much of the dark rye, or *rugbrøt*, in one sitting. *Rugbrøt* is a dense, coarse-ground whole-grain rye bread— the daily bread of Denmark eaten in thin slices with everything imaginable used as topping in a typical way of eating meals or snacks. *Smorrebrød*, literally "butter-bread," is the most elemental example.

Traveling with my friend (and chef at Bar Tartine) Nick Balla, we completely ignored the warnings, wanting to taste as many of the seemingly infinite varieties of *smorrebrød* as possible. At this time I began to understand how whole-grain coarse rye bread is not the easiest thing to digest, and we endured no small discomfort in our quest to taste them all. My favorite rye loaf of the trip, which contained a high percentage of whole rye berries, was made by my friend René Bolvig, a renowned chef in Copenhagen. I was inspired to make a version of this bread—dense with seeds and berries, slightly malty, and impossibly delicious—upon returning to California.

Determined to make something "lighter" in spirit to better suit our coastal California palate, I set about experimenting with making a similar loaf. I began by sprouting the rye berries before adding them to the basic Tartine dough. Adding sprouted grains to bread is not a new idea, of course. As a kid growing up in Texas, I always had the soft sprouted whole-wheat-honey loaves for toast and sandwiches. I loved the texture and subtle sweetness added by the sprouted grains, and didn't even notice I was getting a serving of whole-grain berries in my lunch.

We started to play with this idea at the bakery and found the same gains adding sprouts to an already flavorful, naturally leavened dough destined to become a crusty hearth loaf; we have made dozens of varieties at Tartine. This type of sprout application yields a light and open crumb.

HEARTH LOAVES WITH SPROUTED GRAINS

MASTER METHOD FOR SPROUTING GRAINS

Sprouting grains is simple, and the technique is essentially the same no matter what type of grain you are sprouting. The basic method is to soak the grains in water for 4 to 6 hours. Buckwheat groats are the exception; they should be rinsed two to three times before soaking, then soaked only 20 minutes. Moistening the grain activates the germination process. After soaking, the grain should be thoroughly drained and aerated by lifting and stirring with your hands—because oxygen is required for healthy sprouting to occur. Place the drained sprouts in a clean glass jar or plastic container, cover with cheesecloth, and keep at room temperature; rinse, drain, and aerate the grains twice a day—once in the morning and once in the evening—returning them to the container after each washing. Most grains take 2 to 4 days to sprout depending on the room temperature; warmer is faster, cooler is slower. The grains are ready when they have just sprouted but have not yet formed spider shoots.

Any grain with the endosperm and germ intact will sprout. Notably, pearled barley has been polished in a process that removes or damages parts of the germ and so typically doesn't sprout. Similarly, older varieties of spelt are difficult to hull and can be damaged in the process. Both will still sprout if you use whole, intact grains.

Once the grains sprout, they can be used immediately, kept in the refrigerator in an airtight container for a few days, or frozen for up to a week. Sprouts can also be portioned and vacuum-sealed for storage in the refrigerator. If frozen, thaw in the refrigerator for a couple of days before you want to use them. In the recipes that follow, sprouts are used as a flavoring ingredient, so they are not included in the 100 percent flour amount. All sprouts are added gently after autolyse, about an hour into the bulk rise, when the dough has already developed good structure.

The volume of dry berries approximately doubles after soaking and sprouting. The recipeshere are based on weight measurements for sprouted berries; on average the dry berry weight increases by 65 percent after soaking and sprouting. The slight variation in yield from grain to grain is not an issue, as the percentage of sprouts can be increased or decreased plus or minus 5 percent or more to suit your taste with little effect on the resulting bread. The amount we use in a typical dough is 25 percent, but you could add more; the bread will become more dense with grains as the amount goes up.

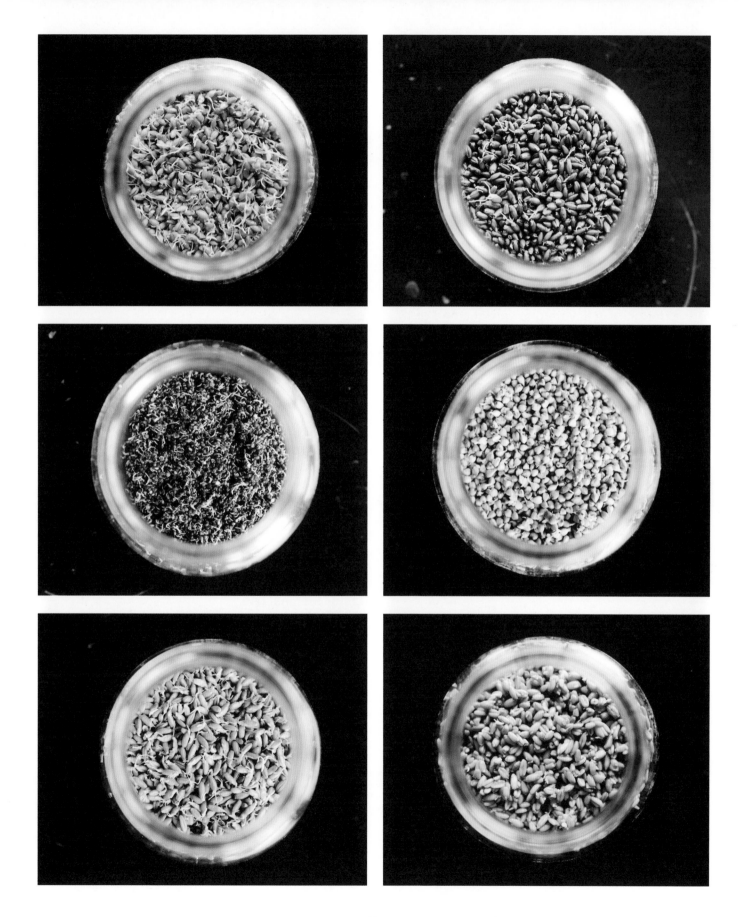

HEARTH LOAVES WITH SPROUTED GRAINS

SPROUTED EINKORN

Einkorn, or small spelt, like the *petit épeautre* I fell for in Provence, is an exceptionally flavorful grain, yet it can produce a weak dough that is not so well suited to my high-hydration and long-rise fermentation technique. But by sprouting these tasty berries and adding them to the dough as a flavoring toward the end of the mix, I was able to create a dough that holds up well throughout the long fermentation period and is full of sweet sprouted-einkorn flavor.

FLOUR	BAKER'S %	WEIGHT
High-extraction wheat flour	40	400 g
Medium-strong wheat flour	40	400 g
Whole-grain einkorn flour	20	200 g
WHEAT GERM	7	70 g
WATER	85	850 g
LEAVEN	15	150 g
FINE SEA SALT	2.5	25 g

ADDITIONS

Sprouted einkorn berries (see page 110)	25	250 g

+ WHEAT BRAN FOR COATING (OPTIONAL)

Follow the master method on page 34 to 37 to make the dough.

After the first two series of turns, about 1 hour into the bulk rise, add the sprouted einkorn berries gently by hand until incorporated into the dough.

Then, follow the instructions for rising, shaping and baking on pages 38 to 41.

Roll the shaped dough in wheat bran to coat. Place in the baskets, bran-side down seam-side up, for the final rise.

Yield: Two loaves

HEARTH LOAVES WITH SPROUTED GRAINS

SPROUTED PURPLE BARLEY

We attempted to sprout blond barley many times for recipes in this book. But, I found that either the germ was damaged when the grain had been polished clean to remove the hard outer layer of the kernel, rendering it unable to sprout, or the hard outer layer of the kernel of unpolished barley remained after sprouting, leaving a tough chewy bit that did not soften after cooking. So we ended up hard toasting the grain and then cooking it for use in a pan bread, and to flavor hearth loaves.

Late in the game, I came across a plump variety of purple barley, and it sprouted beautifully in two days. It found its way into this bread, and is also used in a sprouted pan loaf (see page 146) where it's used as a substitute for rye berries.

FLOUR	BAKER'S %	WEIGHT
Whole Kamut flour	40	400 g
High-extraction wheat flour	30	300 g
Medium-strong bread flour, sifted	30	300 g
WHEAT GERM	7	70 g

WATER	85	850 g
LEAVEN	15	150 g
FINE SEA SALT	2.5	25 g

ADDITIONS		
Sprouted purple barley (see page 110)	25	250 g

+ BARLEY FLAKES FOR COATING (OPTIONAL)

Follow the master method on pages 34 to 37 to make the dough.

After the first two series of turns, about 1 hour into the bulk rise, add the sprouted purple barley gently by hand until incorporated into the dough.

Then, follow the instructions for rising, shaping, and baking on pages 38 to 41.

Roll the shaped dough in barley flakes to coat. Place in the baskets, flake-side down seam-side up, for the final rise.

Yield: Two loaves

HEARTH LOAVES WITH SPROUTED GRAINS

SPROUTED QUINOA-KAMUT

ADDITIONS

Sprouted quinoa (see page 110)	25	250 g

While technically a pseudo-cereal, this Andean "mother of all grains" is widely considered to be a super-food, due to its high protein content and notable concentration of essential nutrients. When sprouted, quinoa takes on a pleasant, slightly green flavor, like that of spinach or beet greens. Quinoa has no gluten, so this flour alone could not be used to make conventional style breads. Sprouted quinoa boosts the overall protein of the loaf, adding with it the complementary flavors of this diverse grain.

+ RAW QUINOA FOR COATING (OPTIONAL)

Follow the master method on page 34 to 37 to make the dough.

After the first two series of turns, about 1 hour into the bulk rise, add the sprouted quinoa gently by hand until incorporated into the dough.

Then, follow the instructions for rising, shaping, and baking on pages 38 to 41.

Roll the shaped dough in raw quinoa to coat. Place in the baskets, quinoa-side down seam-side up, for the final rise.

Yield: Two loaves

FLOUR	BAKER'S %	WEIGHT
Whole Kamut flour	40	400 g
High-extraction wheat flour	30	300 g
Medium-strong wheat flour	30	300 g
WHEAT GERM	7	70 g
WATER	85	850 g
LEAVEN	15	150 g
FINE SEA SALT	2.5	25 g

HEARTH LOAVES WITH SPROUTED GRAINS

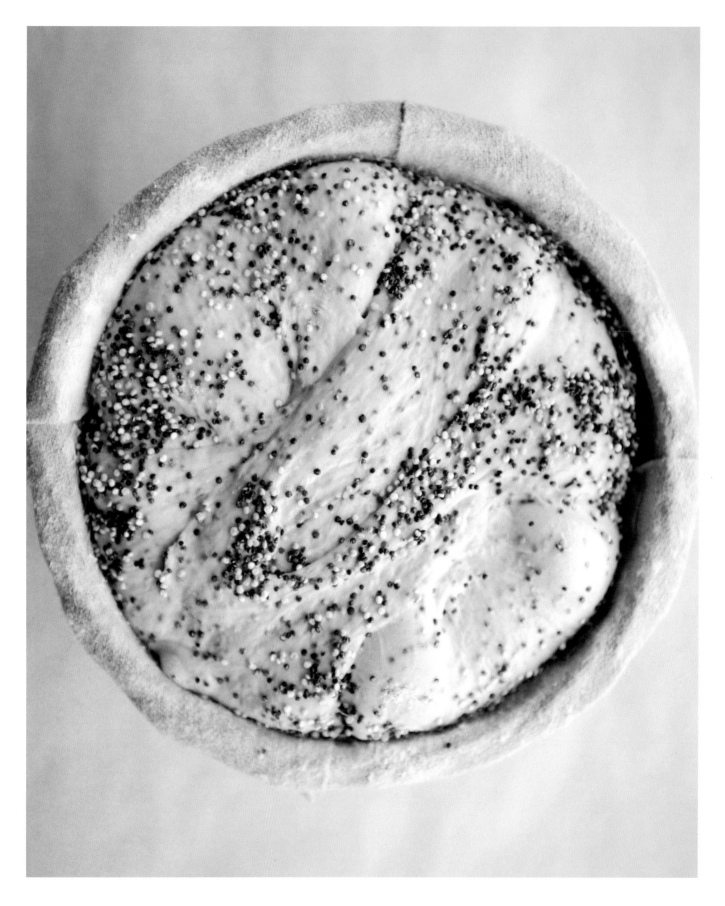

SMOKED SPROUTED RYE

Sprouted rye berries are earthy and sweet. But by using the sprouted grain to flavor the dough, rather than relying on rye flour for structure, I was able to create a loaf with an open, country-style crumb. Be careful to only slightly smoke the sprouted berries so that the result is not overpowering; you want the smoke to complement the other flavors in the bread.

	BAKER'S %	WEIGHT
Alder wood chips		generous 2 handfuls

FLOUR		
Medium-strong wheat flour	50	500 g
Whole-grain wheat flour	20	200 g
High-extraction wheat flour	20	200 g
Whole-grain dark rye flour	10	100 g

WHEAT GERM	7	70 g

WATER	85	850 g

LEAVEN	15	150 g

FINE SEA SALT	2.5	25 g

ADDITIONS

Sprouted rye berries (see page 110)	25	250 g

+ RYE FLAKES FOR COATING (OPTIONAL)

Place the alder wood chips in a heavy-lidded cast-iron pan or wok. Set the pan over high heat until the chips begin to smoke, about 5 minutes. Spread the sprouted grains in an even layer in a steamer basket and place the steamer basket over the chips. Cover with the lid, reduce the heat to low, and smoke for 10 to 15 minutes. Taste the sprouted grains; they should have a distinctly smoky flavor.

Follow the master method on pages 34 to 37 to make the dough.

After the first two series of turns, about 1 hour into the bulk rise, add the smoked sprouted rye berries gently by hand until incorporated into the dough.

Then, follow the instructions for rising, shaping, and baking on pages 38 to 41.

Roll the shaped dough in rye flakes to coat. Place in the baskets, flake-side down seam-side up, for the final rise.

Yield: Two loaves

HEARTH LOAVES WITH SPROUTED GRAINS

SPROUTED KAMUT

Once Kamut berries swell and sprout, they are at least three times the size of einkorn—that is, quite large. So we coarsely grind the sprouted grain before adding it to the dough. At Tartine we use the meat grinder attachment that fits on our mixer. You could also pulse to grind in a food processor. The ground sprouts almost disappear in the dough, receding into the crumb over the long rise and final bake, but the dense, sweet Kamut flavor denotes their presence.

FLOUR	BAKER'S %	WEIGHT
Medium-strong wheat flour	60	600 g
Whole-grain Kamut flour	40	400 g
WHEAT GERM	7	70 g
WATER	85	850 g
LEAVEN	15	150 g
FINE SEA SALT	2.5	25 g

ADDITIONS

Sprouted Kamut berries, coarsely ground (see page 110)	25	250 g

+ KAMUT FLAKES FOR COATING (OPTIONAL)

Follow the master method on pages 34 to 37 to make the dough.

After the first two series of turns, about 1 hour into the bulk rise, add the sprouted Kamut berries gently by hand until incorporated into the dough.

Then, follow the instructions for rising, shaping, and baking on pages 38 to 41.

Roll the shaped dough in Kamut flakes to coat. Place in the baskets flake-side down seam-side up, for the final rise.

Yield: Two loaves

HEARTH LOAVES WITH SPROUTED GRAINS

SPROUTED SPELT

A straightforward bread, the nutty spelt berries add flavor and sumptuous chew.

FLOUR	BAKER'S %	WEIGHT
High-extraction spelt flour	30	300 g
High-extraction wheat flour	30	300 g
Medium-strong wheat flour	30	300 g
Whole spelt flour	10	100 g
WHEAT GERM	7	70 g
WATER	85	850 g
LEAVEN	15	150 g
FINE SEA SALT	2.5	25 g
ADDITIONS		
Sprouted spelt berries (see page 110)	25	250 g

+ SPELT FLAKES FOR COATING (OPTIONAL)

Follow the master method on pages 34 to 37 to make the dough.

After the first two series of turns, about 1 hour into the bulk rise, add the sprouted spelt berries gently by hand until incorporated into the dough.

Then, follow the instructions for rising, shaping, and baking on pages 38 to 41.

Roll the shaped dough in spelt flakes to coat. Place in the baskets flake-side down seam-side up, for the final rise.

Yield: Two loaves

SPROUTED AMARANTH

Similar to quinoa, amaranth is another Andean super-food with high protein and nutritional values. The sprouts lend green notes to the bread, with the savor of collard greens. This specific group of sprouted small "grains"— a family that includes amaranth, quinoa, and millet—impart to the crumb a singular density of flavor bound with texture.

FLOUR	BAKER'S %	WEIGHT
High-extraction wheat flour	50	500 g
Medium-strong wheat flour	50	500 g
WHEAT GERM	7	70 g
WATER	85	850 g
LEAVEN	15	150 g
FINE SEA SALT	2.5	25 g

ADDITIONS

Sprouted amaranth (see page 110)	25	250 g

+ RAW AMARANTH FOR COATING (OPTIONAL)

Follow the master method on pages 34 to 37 to make the dough.

After the first two series of turns, about 1 hour into the bulk rise, add the sprouted amaranth gently by hand until incorporated into the dough.

Then, follow the instructions for rising, shaping, and baking on pages 38 to 41.

Roll the shaped dough in raw amaranth to coat. Place in the baskets, amaranth-side down seam-side up, for the final rise.

Yield: Two loaves

HEARTH LOAVES WITH SPROUTED GRAINS

HEARTH LOAVES WITH SPROUTED GRAINS

SPROUTED BUCKWHEAT

One can't use much more than 5 percent buck-wheat flour in a conventional bread dough before the loaf starts trending flat during the bake. Buckwheat has plenty of flavor, but no gluten. The taste is intense and distinct, lending its earthy savor to everything it goes into. To make a Tartine-style country loaf with buckwheat, we've employed a few different techniques. For this bread, we first sprout the groats as they soften and the seeds begin their transformation into plants.

This bread is distinct from the bread that contains toasted groats (see page 54) in that it has a slightly sweeter flavor contributed by the sprouted grain. The range of the three breads is a good example of how we have learned to broaden the flavor profile of these extraordinary grains by approaching them much as we would if we were preparing an egg or a bunch of asparagus—eating the ingredient raw and then cooking it in various ways. The results are all markedly different.

FLOUR	BAKER'S %	WEIGHT
Medium-strong wheat flour	70	700 g
Whole-grain wheat flour	30	300 g
WHEAT GERM	7	70 g
WATER	85	850 g
LEAVEN	15	150 g
FINE SEA SALT	2.5	25 g

ADDITIONS

Sprouted buckwheat groats (see page 110)	30	300 g

+ COARSELY GROUND BUCKWHEAT GROATS FOR COATING (OPTIONAL)

Follow the master method on pages 34 to 37 to make the dough.

After the first two series of turns, about 1 hour into the bulk rise, add the sprouted buckwheat groats gently by hand until incorporated into the dough.

Then, follow the instructions for rising, shaping, and baking on pages 38 to 41.

Roll the shaped dough in ground buckwheat groats to coat. Place in the baskets groat-side down seam-side up, for the final rise.

Yield: Two loaves

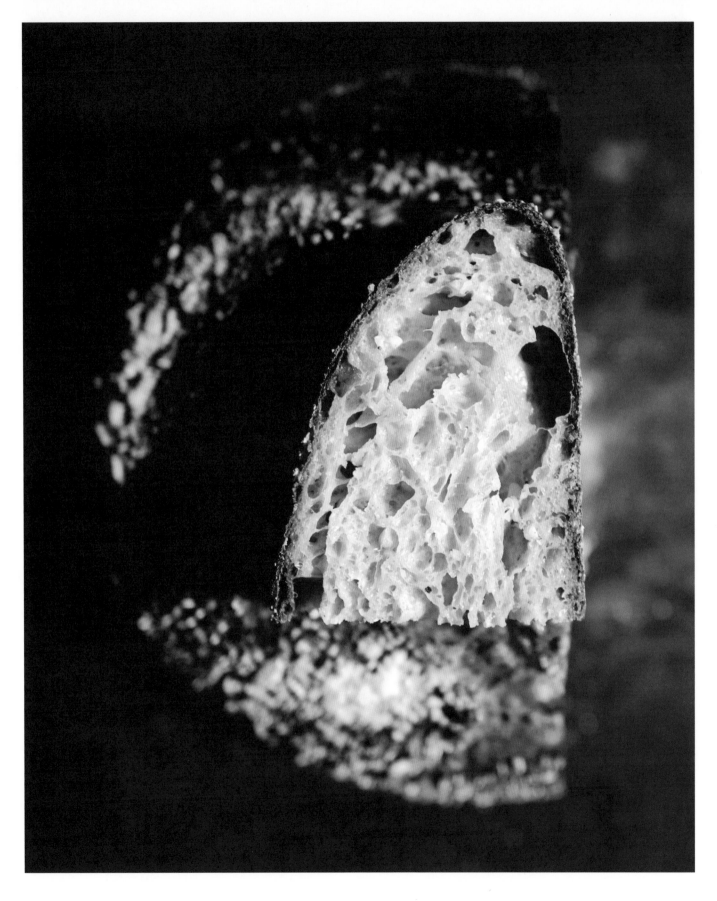

SPROUTED EMMER WITH MAPLE & BEER

The notion here was to create a hearth bread with a flavor akin to the René's Rye (page 140). Eventually we settled on a different, decidedly manifest way to achieve this (see pages 138 to 139). But we liked the flavor of this early effort; while not so close to René's, it had its own appeal. This is a hearty, rich bread with ancient grain savor—the flavor of the beer is balanced by sweet, subtle maple.

FLOUR	BAKER'S %	WEIGHT
Whole-grain emmer flour	30	300 g
High-extraction wheat flour	30	300 g
Medium-strong bread flour	20	200 g
Whole-grain wheat flour	20	200 g
Raw wheat germ	7	70 g
Light beer	30	300 g
Maple syrup	7	70 g

WATER	50	500 g
LEAVEN	15	150 g
FINE SEA SALT	2.5	25 g

ADDITIONS		
Sprouted emmer (see page 110)	25	250 g

Follow the master method on pages 34 to 37 to make the dough, adding the beer and maple syrup to the water in the water-leaven mixture.

After the first two series of turns, about 1 hour into the bulk rise, add the sprouted emmer gently by hand until incorporated into the dough.

Then, follow the instructions for rising, shaping, and baking on pages 38 to 41.

Yield: Two loaves

HEARTH LOAVES WITH SPROUTED GRAINS

RENÉ'S-STYLE PAN LOAVES

My initial deconstructing of the traditional Danish-style rye bread, *rugbrød*, began with increasing the percentage of whole rye berries in the recipe and sprouting them. Following that, I started shifting ratios, and along the way a metatheory of the formula led to a few different readings of the same composition; the recipes that follow in this section illustrate the different directions you could take this style of bread.

Unlike the sprouted hearth loaves in the preceding pages, René's-style pan loaves have a large percentage of whole sprouted berries and a comparatively small percentage of flour, much of it low-gluten. Therefore, these doughs will look and feel different from the mixed-grain hearth loaves. Though different, the basic timeline for making them remains the same as the hearth loaves. But since the pan breads are much denser, they are baked longer at a lower temperature to ensure that they are fully baked before the outside crust burns.

MASTER METHOD FOR
SPROUTED-GRAIN PAN LOAVES

All our sprouted-grain recipes contain a larger percentage of non-flour ingredients. Therefore in order to maintain a yield of two loaves, we've scaled the flour in all these recipes to 500 grams rather than 1 kilogram.

To mix the sprouted-grain pan breads, first measure the flours and put in a large bowl. In a second large bowl, combine all of the liquids and leaven and mix by hand to incorporate. Add the flour to the water-leaven mixture and mix by hand until thoroughly combined, about 5 minutes. Let the dough rest, covered, in the bowl for 30 minutes. Add the salt, sprouted grains, and seeds and continue mixing by hand until incorporated. The dough should have the feel of wet concrete.

Cover the bowl with a clean kitchen towel and let rise at warm room temperature (80 to 85°F/ 26 to 29°C) for about 3 hours, giving it folds every 45 minutes to strengthen the dough (see page 38). Dip your hands in water (to prevent the dough from sticking), and scoop the dough into twice-buttered steel pans, which prevents the loaves from sticking. At Tartine we use both standard-size and miniature (4 by 6 in/ 10 by 15 cm) loaf pans. Alternately, use nonstick loaf pans. Smooth the tops of the loaves with wet hands. Let rise in the pans, uncovered, for 2 hours more at warm room temperature. Cover the pans with a clean, dry kitchen towel and let rise overnight in the refrigerator.

The next day, when you're ready to bake, use a pair of scissors to make shallow cuts in the tops of the loaves to score, brush with water, and bake at 425°F/220°C for 1 hour and 15 to 25 minutes, or until the internal temperature has reached 210°F/100°C. Due to the very high overall hydration of these doughs, it's essential to bake them thoroughly. Let cool on a wire rack for at least half a day before cutting. Typically, I wait until the next day to cut into the bread, as the crumb is very moist and the resting times make it easier to slice this bread thinly. These breads keep well for up to one week properly wrapped or in a bread box.

RENÉ'S RYE

This hearty bread came together quickly, as I started with a base recipe generously given to me by my Danish chef friend René Bolvig. My formula changed and evolved over time to be something quite different from the original, but the loaf itself—a nutrient-dense brick of sprouted grains and seeds—holds true to the source. Sprouting the grain makes the bread immensely more digestible, and adds a natural sweetness from the rye berries themselves. We use beer made by our friends at Linden Street Brewery in Oakland, who ferment the brew using our natural bread starter as the sole culture. The buttermilk and whey used in these loaves is what's left after our weekly production of fresh cheese and butter at Bar Tartine. The loaf can also be shaved into thin slices and baked to make lacy crisps.

WATER	95	475 g
LEAVEN	62	310 g
FINE SEA SALT	3.5	17 g

DRY ADDITIONS

Sprouted rye berries (see page 110)	105	525 g
Sunflower seeds	9	45 g
Whole brown flaxseeds	27	135 g
Coarsely ground brown flaxseeds	13	70 g
Unhulled brown sesame seeds	21	105 g
Pumpkin seeds	9	45 g

FLOUR

	BAKER'S %	WEIGHT
High-extraction spelt flour	80	400 g
Whole-grain dark rye flour	20	100 g

WET ADDITIONS

Buttermilk	36	180 g
Dark beer	27	135 g
Dark malt syrup	4	20 g

Follow the master method for sprouted grain pan loaves on page 138 to make the dough. Then, follow the instructions for rising, shaping, and baking on page 139.

Yield: Two loaves

RENÉ'S-STYLE PAN LOAVES

RENÉ'S-STYLE PAN LOAVES

TOASTED BARLEY

One of the first breads I learned to make from Richard Bourdon was his brown rice bread, in which a large portion of cooked and cooled brown rice was added to the dough toward the end of the mix. The bread was exceptionally moist, slightly sweet from the rice, and loaded with whole grain. I had already planned to include a brown rice bread recipe (see page 186) as homage to Bourdon's bread so, with cooked grain in mind, I swapped barley for rye for this bread. Instead of sprouting, the barley is toasted and cooked before being added to the dough.

	BAKER'S %	WEIGHT
Whole barley berries, toasted (see page 190)		400 g
Cold water		800 g
FLOUR		
High-extraction spelt flour	80	400 g
Whole einkorn flour	20	100 g
WET ADDITIONS		
Buttermilk	36	180 g
Light beer	27	135 g
Dark malt syrup	4	20 g
WATER	95	475 g

LEAVEN	62	310 g
FINE SEA SALT	3.5	17 g
ADDITIONS		
Cooked, cooled barley	105	525 g
Golden flaxseeds	41	205 g
Sesame seeds	21	105 g
Pumpkin seeds	9	45 g
Sunflower seeds	9	45 g
Golden raisins, soaked in hot water for 15 minutes, then drained (optional)	30	150 g

Place the toasted barley berries in a medium saucepan and add the cold water. Bring to a boil over high heat, then reduce the heat so the water is simmering, cover, and simmer for 30 to 40 minutes, until the barley has absorbed all of the cooking liquid. Remove from the heat, transfer the cooked grain to a baking sheet, and let cool completely.

Follow the master method for sprouted grain pan loaves on page 138 to make the dough, adding the buttermilk, beer, and malt syrup to the water in the water-leaven mixture. Add the cooked barley at the same time as you add the seeds, raisins, and salt. Then, follow the instructions for rising, shaping, and baking on page 139.

Yield: Two loaves

RENÉ'S-STYLE PAN LOAVES

PURPLE BARLEY AMAZAKE

Amazake is a naturally sweet rice porridge. Made in Japan for over a thousand years, rice is cultured with Aspergillus oryzae mold, which converts the starch into sugars. Undiluted amazake is very sweet, often diluted with water to make a traditional grain drink, so it seemed a perfect whole-food sweetener to use in place of barley malt syrup in bread. Prepared amazake is available in Japanese markets and online. Amazake with sprouted barley yields a bread with a complex blend of diverse grain flavors.

FLOUR	BAKER'S %	WEIGHT
High-extraction spelt flour	80	400 g
Dark rye flour	20	100 g
WATER	95	475 g
LEAVEN	62	310 g

WET ADDITIONS		
Prepared sweet amazake	20	100 g
Dark beer	27	135 g
Buttermilk	36	180 g
FINE SEA SALT	3.5	17 g

DRY ADDITIONS		
Sprouted purple barley (see page 110)	105	525 g
Brown flaxseeds	41	205 g
Brown sesame seeds	21	105 g
Sunflower seeds	9	45 g
Pumpkin seeds	9	45 g

Follow the master method for sprouted grain pan loaves on page 138 to make the dough, adding the amazake, beer, and buttermilk to the water in the water-leaven mixture. Add the sprouted barley and the seeds at the same time as you add the salt.

Then, follow the instructions for rising, shaping, and baking on page 139.

Yield: Two loaves

147 RENÉ'S-STYLE PAN LOAVES

RENÉ'S-STYLE PAN LOAVES

SPROUTED BUCKWHEAT–EINKORN

Sprouted rye berries are replaced with whole sprouted buckwheat groats, and whole-grain einkorn flour is used instead of spelt. The bread is sweetened again with sweet amazake made from cultured rice. This bread has primordial depths of ancient flavor; it was the last recipe we made before going to print.

FLOUR	BAKER'S %	WEIGHT
Whole-grain einkorn flour	80	400 g
Buckwheat flour	20	100 g

WET ADDITIONS		
Buttermilk	36	180 g
Light beer	27	135 g
Prepared sweet amazake	20	100 g

WATER	95	475 g

LEAVEN	62	310 g

FINE SEA SALT	3.5	17 g

DRY ADDITIONS

Sprouted buckwheat groats (see page 110)	105	525 g
Sunflower seeds	9	45 g
Whole brown flaxseeds	41	205 g
Unhulled sesame seeds	21	105 g
Pumpkin seeds	9	45 g

Follow the master method for sprouted grain pan loaves on page 138 to make the dough, adding the buttermilk, beer, and amazake to the water in the water-leaven mixture. Add the sprouted buckwheat groats and seeds at the same time as you add the salt.

Then, follow the instructions for rising, shaping, and baking on page 139.

Yield: Two loaves

RENÉ'S-STYLE PAN LOAVES

RENÉ'S
META LOAF

After testing many complex recipe configu-
rations in the quest to produce a hearth loaf
with the flavor profile of our sprouted Rene's
pan loaf, one of our bakers suggested the
obvious that had not occurred to me. Why not
just grate a loaf of Rene's Rye and add it to
the dough like we're doing with all these other
grains? Obvious and brilliant. There is certainly
precedent for adding baked bread to fresh
doughs in rye baking tradition; our take on
the technique worked just as we'd hoped.

ADDITIONS

	BAKER'S %	WEIGHT
René's Rye (page 140), crust removed and coarsely grated on a box grater	25	250 g

Follow the master method on pages 34 to 37 to make the dough.

After the first two series of turns, about 1 hour into the bulk rise, add the coarsely grated René's Rye gently by hand until incorporated into the dough.

Then, follow the instructions for rising, shaping, and baking on pages 38 to 41.

Yield: Two loaves

FLOUR	BAKER'S %	WEIGHT
Medium-strong bread flour	55	550 g
Whole-grain white wheat flour	30	300 g
High-extraction whole-wheat flour	15	150 g
WHEAT GERM	7	70 g
WATER	85	850 g
LEAVEN	15	150 g
FINE SEA SALT	2.5	25 g

153 RENÉ'S-STYLE PAN LOAVES

GERMANY & AUSTRIA

My friend and de facto European travel advisor, Kille Enna, is half German and half Danish. I was planning another research trip to Europe, thinking I'd head back to Copenhagen, where enthusiasm for bread baking was building, to meet up with her. Kille, who frequently writes for German food magazines and recently had one of her cookbooks published in Germany, suggested we check out the Bavarian bread scene in southern Germany, a region renowned for its hearty rye and wheat breads, much of it naturally leavened and made with whole grains.

Kille was keen on introducing me to her friend Georg Schweisfurth, known as Geo, a Munich native with whom Kille felt a close kinship, saying, "Had I been born a man, this is the one I'd be." Geo was a strapping Bavarian gentleman with a naturally informed taste for fine art and food. His father had at one time

experiment called *Kunst geht in die Fabrik*. Geo's father taught his son the butchery trade but, after a point, Geo's father tired of the factory and sold it, deciding to instead create a farm based on a philosophy of a compassionate, "shepherding" style of animal husbandry. Agriculture would be a key part of the new project, as they would grow good food for the animals on the property. After much research and planning, the radically sustainable farm called Hermannsdorfer, located just outside of Munich, came to be in 1985.

Geo, along with his brother, worked to build the family vision. Hermannsdorfer is renowned, among other things, for raising an heirloom breed of pig that mostly feeds on wild meadow plants and digs in the dirt for roots and worms. These pigs develop a distinct flavor and fat character, and are used to make the prized

Rauris, Austria

owned the largest sausage factory in Europe, where he had (in)famously hosted renowned modern artists, allowing them to create installations and murals within the slaughterhouse as a public and social art study in the 1960s. There was a book published to chronicle this bone-in cured Bavarian hams that age for two to three years before consumption, like Italian prosciutto or Spanish pata negra.

Over the years other projects followed. Hermannsdorfer now has a bakery, restaurant, and retail shop that sells organic and

relative to the bread I was making at Tartine, made from a very wet dough with a dark-baked crackling crust. Along the way, I figured I'd stop to visit Le Boulangerie Savoyarde nearby, and say hello to old friends I had worked with apprenticing under Patrick LePort. From there, I'd head to Munich to meet Kille and Geo.

It all seemed so close on the map. After landing in Geneva, locating a car to rent proved much more diffi-cult than I had anticipated. The day I arrived apparently marked the beginning of a holiday weekend, and cars for hire were scarce all over the region. Plus it had started to pour

Georg Schweisfurth

biodynamic groceries, fresh meat, and traditional German sausages. The bakery stone-grinds flour daily and bakes bread in massive ovens attached to the restaurant, which serves food from the farm in a pro-gressive, modern German style. These days, Geo manages a charming inn built in 1901, situated nearby, called Sonnenhausen. He is gradually transforming the grounds of Sonnenhausen into a nature preserve focused on celebrating the biodiversity of Bavarian plants and wild animals, and continues to be active in Basic, the company he founded in 1997, a visionary small chain of stylish, certified organic food markets.

Kille contacted Geo to see if he'd be in town when we were passing through. He was, and mentioned a wood-fired-oven bread festival, the Brotfest, that would be happening in two

rain across the Alps. The German language GPS was no use, and iPhone navigation while driving on the autobahn through mountain storms was not going to happen. After living in California for so many years, I often forget to factor the weather properly into my plans. Best

weeks' time in Austria, a few hours drive from Munich into the Alps. He would be attending, and offered to arrange for me to work with fresh-milled biodynamic Austrian grain as the American guest baker of the festival, which included bakers from across Austria. He also arranged a visit to the workshop where the renowned Austrian stone mills are made, still family owned and operated by father and daughter. This was quite short notice, but such a generous offer seemed too perfect a situation to pass up.

Looking at maps to plan in haste, I had all sorts of notions. The half-baked idea I settled on was to fly into Geneva and drive across the Alps, stopping in the city of Basel to find a bread I had seen in a Richemont Craft School baking book while I was studying at the Culinary Institute of America and simultaneously apprenticing for Richard Bourdon in the Berkshires.

The Basel bread I spotted in the book had been an imagined case scenario: The rain would slow me down a lot. It quickly became clear that it would be impossible to make it to Munich on time.

Anxious, I spent the next morning walking around Geneva tasting breads and flew that afternoon to Munich. There I'd have a couple of days to revive my hibernating bread starter before the Brotfest in Austria. Breads in Switzerland are distinct and range widely across regions, called cantons. I wasn't going to discover the mythical Basel bread that day in Geneva.

After settling in Munich and feeding my starter at the hotel, I headed to the Manufactum to meet Kille and Geo. Manufactum is one of

Hermannsdorfer hogs feasting on clover

Kille's favorite stores. "The good things still exist" is the phrase printed on each takeaway bag. Manufactum, which means "handmade" in German, carries all sorts of artisanal products from around the world, including a choice selection of kitchen supplies. I picked up a

from the same foundation. But coming from a place like America, which has no bread dogma, has its benefits. I was free to choose which traditions to study and the mentors I wanted to learn from. Even after forty years of baking, my first teacher, Richard Bourdon, is always tinkering with techniques to get him closer to his ideal loaf. His open-mindedness, along with a mercurial tendency to change philosophical procla- mations about how and why we were doing this or that, made a strong impres- sion on me that per- sists to this day: There will always be a lot more to learn.

In Austria, after settling in with a handful of talented and generous bakers at Brotfest, I noted

Herrmannsdorfer ham

hand-cranked circular slicer used to cut very thin slices of German (or Danish) whole-grain rye bread. Inside Manufactum is a small bakery called Brot and Butter, known for its Bavarian rye bread made with freshly milled biodynamic wheat and rye. This bread is used as the base for open-faced sandwiches, similar to Danish smørrebrød. For breakfast, I enjoyed a simple slice of fresh bread spread with butter paired with a cup of strong coffee. It was the perfect, restorative manna to my soul searching: I was back on track.

Kille's husband, Morten, joined us in Munich. From there, our foursome made our way to Rauris, Austria, a small town in the Alps, to attend the Brotfest. Kille has always been like my sharp, overachieving twin sister. Geo was now the cool uncle: master butcher and chef, smart modern-art collector, black diamond alpine skier, founder of visionary organic food markets—the guy even makes lederhosen chic. We were fast friends. The

a similar use and treatment of the natural leaven to what I had seen in Copenhagen. The leaven was kept generally quite sour, left between feedings for long stretches and used more as a dough conditioner and flavoring component than a leavening agent. The primary leavener was commercial yeast, or something in between commercial yeast and sourdough called *backferment* that is popular in Germany, Austria, and Denmark. *Backferment* is a dry granulated isolate of wild yeasts and lactic acid bacteria made from honey. It produces results similar to sourdough but is typically less sour and lower in acid.

My technique for using young leaven produced similar results as the *backferment*. Adding it to the bread dough while young, before it develops a pronounced acidity, was definitely not a part of the regional Austrian bread tradition.

Of course, I could understand the popularity of using *backferment*. The labor required to maintain a truly leavening natural leaven is a never-ending cycle. And yet, it's still only a small, if key part of the relentless attention to detail that is required to maintain consistent results. The rest is shifting daily: Scores of factors, such as temperature and humidity, changes in the flour from harvest to harvest, weather conditions, and the living nature of the dough have to be taken

Mill in Bavaria

The rains continued; Geo and Morten did the driving as I took in the dramatic alpine scenery. Speeding through mountain passes, the thought occurred to me that I really didn't know what I was getting myself into. My leaven, which I'd brought with me from San Francisco, was in good shape, though; I knew the flour I'd be working with was high-quality, and I had used wood-fired ovens for half of my baking life. I was basically trading my coastal setting for the mountains: the inverse of what I had done twenty years prior, when I finished my apprenticeship at Patrick LePort's bakery in the Savoie to settle on the coast of Northern California. Again, I was bringing my own methods to a place with a historical bread tradition, one as strong as in France and Denmark.

In countries with the strongest bread tradition, a world of knowledge is handed down from generation to generation for centuries. Master techniques for growing and milling grain are preserved. None of the techniques I use now would exist without my having first studied this tradition, and all are derived

flavor without developing overpowering acid during the extensive stages of fermentation.

I met this same dogma of tradition with my beloved mentor Patrick LePort, who to this day makes some of the finest bread I have ever tasted. He uses a young leaven to raise his exceptional baguettes. The last time we met in Brittany, I noted how his young leaven was similar to the one I use at home for all my breads. He told me this type of leaven would not work for normal breads, with the yoke of tradition backing his certain tone, even though I'd been making bread successfully with young leaven for years.

The bread I made in Austria had more flavor than much of what I'd been making at home: Open textured with a glistening crumb and a sweet fermented aroma, it was Tartine-style bread that just tasted better. It was becoming clear that these other bread-eating countries

Mixing dough by hand, Austria

into account throughout the day while making bread.

It was late summer in the mountains, with hot, sunny days and cool nights, perfect conditions for maintaining my lively leaven. I was given bags of excellent, freshly milled biodynamic wheat and rye flours and set to mixing my doughs by hand, just as I had done in Point Reyes. Two of the Austrian bakers brought small wood-fired ovens on trailers they used to make bread at festivals throughout the year and offered to share oven space. We set up tables in the morning, and by noon I was shaping bread. The Austrian bakers were certainly friendly, but there was a language barrier: None of them spoke English.

In Denmark, though the dense rye breads are cast in tradition, the artisan wheat–bread movement is a modern phenomenon, which explains in part the Danish bakers' open

were growing much more flavorful grain than I had access to.

If it's possible to be both encouraged and discouraged at once, that's how I left Austria. I'd just made some of the best loaves of bread of my career, and I knew that I wouldn't be able to achieve the same results at home unless I found a source for the same quality and variety of freshly milled grains.

I returned to California determined to forge new relationships with pioneering farmers who were committed to growing more flavorful varieties of grains and millers who would be willing to mill these grains into flour.

On the train to Osttiroler Getreidemühlen, Austria

enthusiasm for new techniques. In Austria, by contrast, my method of using young leaven was met with sharp skepticism. The idea of using a sourdough leaven at this stage, before it had developed a very pronounced acidity, was alien to their tradition, as was the notion of such a long final rise. They simply didn't believe that I could make good bread with this method. But my years of experimentation in California had taught me that, especially when using more volatile freshly milled whole-grain flours to make breads, young leaven is essential to achieving full

PORRIDGE, CRACKED-, AND FLAKED-GRAIN BREADS

After *Tartine Bread* was finished, I began revisiting the world of whole grains. I wanted to go beyond what is typically done when approaching this family of breads, which is to replace some or all of the refined flour in a recipe with whole-grain flour. Breads made only with high-gluten whole-grain flours can be tough and have a bitter flavor, or in turn be heavy and dull, weighed down by the coarse fiber of the bran. This is one of the reasons I drifted away from making whole-grain bread, but the flavors of the grains themselves kept drawing me back. Many types of flour, particularly ancient and heirloom grains, are too weak to be effectively used as the majority grain to make a free-form loaf of bread; use too high of a percentage and the texture, overall crumb, and crust of the loaf begin to suffer. Thus most whole-grain breads are made with a small variety of suitable grains, resulting in the narrow range of whole-grain breads generally available.

The idea struck while reading a chapter in our friend Sandor Katz's inspired and exhaustive manual, *The Art of Fermentation*. At the bakery, we had recently left a soaked cereal mix out for a few days before using it in a test bread. I liked the pleasantly mild, fresh, cheeselike aromas that developed as the soaked grain started to ferment before we added it to the final dough.

How much more whole grain could I get into the dough and how much more digestible could I make it by prefermenting? The question that goes deepest to the heart of the matter was illuminated years ago by my iconic chef-mentor at the Culinary Institute of America, George Higgins: How much flavor could I add? Higgins told me, "There is a fifth flavor the Japanese call umami and it's powerful." Natural fermentation is one way to bring out a broad range of umami flavors. Chef Higgins predicted a future trend in all things fermented.

While at the CIA, I was obsessed with natural leavened bread, at the time moonlighting with Richard Bourdon at Berkshire Mountain Bakery to the detriment of everything else at culinary school to which I was supposed to be applying myself. Chef Higgins could see that I had dived deep, and seeing the prospect of no return, he encouraged me to continue on.

Through considerable experimentation with my team at Tartine, I developed alternative approaches to using whole grains. Sprouting grains before adding them to the dough was one such method we built different techniques on. Cooking grains into a porridge that gets folded into the dough was another discovery, and fermenting these same porridge grains for a day or two before using resulted in loaves with a depth of flavor I had never tasted, without sacrificing many of the aesthetic and textural qualities I love about Tartine bread.

The porridge method and, to some extent, the sprouted grain method also make it possible to add a larger percentage of grains with very low or no gluten, such as barley, oats, and coarse rye (pumpernickel), so the flavor of the specific grain is evident, while still achieving a loaf with a moist, pearlescent open crumb and substantial crust. The signature Tartine style is preserved, even while incorporating upward of 50 percent or more grains that are not typically suited to making hearth breads. For me, this represents a sort of third wave for whole-grain breads, adding a new range and depth of flavors while maintaining ideal structure and volume.

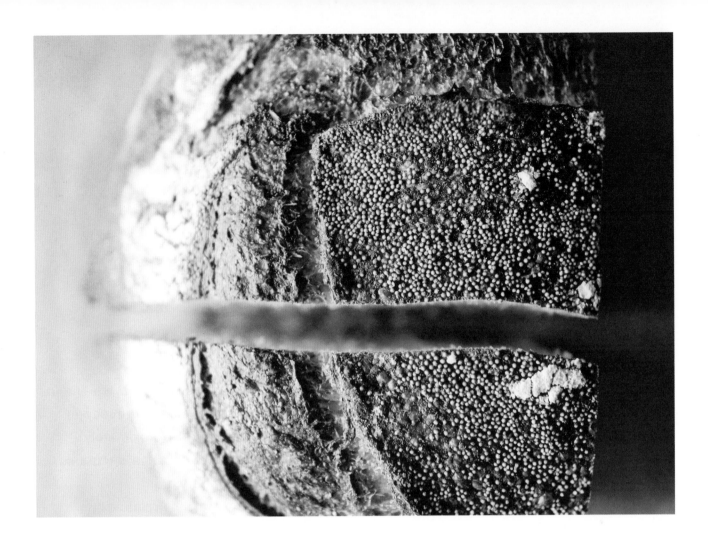

Cooking whole or coarsely ground or cracked grains renders them more easily digestible; the porridge is incorporated into the dough toward the end of the mixing process, after the dough has been properly developed. Rather than replacing a percentage of the flour with these grains, they are added as you would nuts, dried fruit, or seeds, as a flavoring agent rather than a part of the overall flour blend.

When they emerge from the oven, the superhydrated porridge breads are barely set, so much so that I generally let the bread carefully cool overnight before cutting into it. The trade-off for patience is shelf life: A loaf of porridge bread will easily keep a week before it stales. The first time I made these breads, they seemed an ultimate expression of whole-grain baking. They retain the delicate, nuanced flavors of the ancient grains but in a loaf of bread that has a tender crumb and substantial crust.

MASTER METHOD
FOR PORRIDGE BREADS

These recipes include 50 percent cooked, cooled porridge based on 100 percent total flour weight. Fifty percent is a high enough percentage to ensure that you taste the grain used, and is a starting point that yields good results, though you could use a larger or smaller percentage. Use more porridge and the bread will get moister and more dense; use less porridge and the flavor of the grain is reduced. Porridge doughs are mixed using a lower base hydration (75 percent), as the cooked porridge introduces more hydration when added.

Grains used to make porridge are cracked, rolled, or flaked; cooked with a 2-to-1 ratio of water to grain; and seasoned with salt. The method is the same regardless of the grain you are using.

To prepare porridge, combine 2 parts water and 1 part flaked or cracked grains in a saucepan over medium heat. To make approximately 500 grams of cooked porridge, use 500 grams of water to 250 grams of dry grain. Cook, stirring occasionally, until the grains soften and become creamy, about 15 minutes. Whole, uncracked grains take longer to cook, which is why we either use flaked or rolled grains or crack the grains before cooking them (see page 170). Season with salt. Spread the cooked porridge in a thin layer on a baking sheet to cool before using in a bread recipe. The cooked grains can be stored, covered, in the refrigerator for up to a week; bring back to room temperature before adding to the dough.

I've paired each porridge bread with a complementary toasted nut and nut oil to make a flavored porridge bread. But if you choose to omit the nuts and nut oil, the plain porridge breads are delicious on their own.

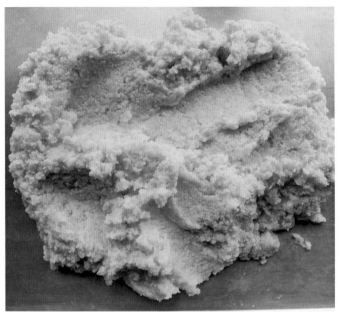

You also have the option of prefermenting the uncooked porridge grains for a day or two before cooking them, which will contribute more flavor and render the grains more digestible. I call this "double fermented," as the grains are first fermented separately, then for a second time in the bread dough. To do this, dissolve 1 teaspoon of young leaven (see page 35) in 500 grams of water and add 250 grams of grains, stirring to incorporate. Cover and leave out at cool room temperature overnight, then cook the grains into porridge (in the same water in which they soaked) and proceed with the bread recipe. Alternatively, one could use fresh whey or live culture yogurt to inoculate the grains instead of leaven. I have used fresh whey for all or a portion of the liquid (maintaining 500 grams as the total liquid weight), and when using yogurt to inoculate, I use the same amount as the young leaven. All three will start lactic fermentation.

The basic dough for the porridge dough is made using the Master Method for Tartine Loaves (page 30), with reduced hydration (750 grams water instead of 850 grams). After the first two series of turns, about 1 hour into the bulk rise, add the cooked, cooled porridge by hand until incorporated into the dough. Follow the instructions for rising, shaping, and baking the loaves on pages 38 to 41.

MASTER METHOD FOR CRACKED- AND FLAKED-GRAIN BREADS

These cracked grain bread recipes include 50 percent soaked and fermented cracked grain based on 100 percent total flour weight. Fifty percent is a high enough percentage to ensure that you taste the grain used and is a good starting point that yields good results, through you could use a larger or smaller percentage.

You can soak coarsely chopped flakes, including oats, barley, rye, and spelt, or cracked whole-grain berries. To prepare flaked grains, put them in the bowl of a food processor and pulse until coarsely chopped. Whole-grain berries should be coarsely cracked using a home grain mill (or mill attachment for a stand mixer) or a powerful blender. After the grains are cracked, place them in a sifter to separate the finer flour; reserve this and use it to coat the exterior of your formed loaves to prevent them from sticking to the cloth lining the baskets during the long rise.

Once the grains have been coarsely chopped or cracked, soak them in water, using a ratio of 2 parts water to 1 part grain. For oats, use a 3-to-1 ratio, as oats absorb more water. To make approximately 500 grams of soaked fermented cracked or flaked grain, use 500 grams of water to 250 grams of dry cracked or flaked grain (750 grams of water to 250 grams of flaked oats). Put the water and grain in a bowl and stir to combine. You also have the option of pre-fermenting the uncooked, flaked, or cracked grains, as with the porridge breads. Add 1 table-spoon of natural leaven (see page 35), yogurt, or fresh whey to the soaking liquid, stirring to incorporate. As with the prefermented porridge bread technique (see page 169), I refer to this as "double fermented," since you are first fermenting the grains on their own, then again once they've been added to the dough. Cover and let sit for 1 to 2 days at room temperature. After a couple of days the fermentation from souring will be mild and the grains will have softened and absorbed most of

the water. Let soak longer if you want a stronger fermented flavor. I look for a beerlike aroma to develop before using the cracked rye to make our pumpernickel, which typically takes about 3 days (stirring each day) in our warm bakeshop.

Once you are ready to use the soaked grains in the dough, strain off the excess liquid, using a fine-mesh colander. The soaked grain can be stored in the refrigerator, covered, or vacuum-sealed for up to three days.

The basic dough for cracked and flaked grains is made using the Master Method for Tartine Loaves (page 30), with reduced hydration (750 grams water instead of 850 grams). After the first two series of turns, about 1 hour into the bulk rise, add the cracked, soaked (prefermented) grains by hand until incorporated into the dough. Then, follow the instructions for rising, shaping, and baking the loaves on pages 38 to 41.

RYE PORRIDGE

Cooked rye porridge introduces a fresh layer of rye flavor, distinct from that of rye flour and sprouted rye berries in its earthiness. The rye flakes are soaked overnight until slightly soured before being cooked into a porridge. Rye has high levels of pentosan vegetable gums that gel to bind water as the grain is cooked, giving the crumb a striking succulence. Again, this technique allows for a large portion of low-gluten whole-grain to be added to a hearth-style country loaf with no negative impact on the volume or open texture of the crumb.

FLOUR	BAKER'S %	WEIGHT
High-extraction wheat flour	50	500 g
Medium-strong wheat flour	50	500 g
WHEAT GERM	7	70 g
WATER	75	750 g
LEAVEN	15	150 g
FINE SEA SALT	2.5	25 g

ADDITIONS

Cooked rye flake porridge (see page 168), cooled	50	500 g
Walnuts, toasted and coarsely chopped (optional)	25	250 g
Walnut oil (optional)	5	50 g

+ RYE FLAKES FOR COATING (OPTIONAL)

Follow the master method on pages 34 to 37 to make the dough.

After the first two series of turns, about 1 hour into the bulk rise, add the rye porridge, walnuts, and walnut oil gently by hand until incorporated into the dough.

Then, follow the instructions for rising, shaping, and baking on pages 38 to 41

Roll the shaped dough in rye flakes to coat. Place in the baskets, flake-side down seam-side up, for the final rise.

Yield: Two loaves

KAMUT PORRIDGE–GOLDEN FLAX

Kamut is about 30 percent higher in protein than modern wheat. Cooking Kamut flakes as you would oatmeal transforms the grain into a nutritious golden yellow porridge. The addition of flax—another ingredient high in natural vegetable gums—adds moist body to the bread.

FLOUR	BAKER'S %	WEIGHT
High-extraction wheat flour	50	500 g
Medium-strong wheat flour	50	500 g
WHEAT GERM	7	70 g
WATER	75	750 g
LEAVEN	15	150 g
FINE SEA SALT	2.5	25 g

PORRIDGE

Cooked Kamut-flake porridge, with golden flaxseeds added near end of cooking, cooled (see page 168)	50	500 g
Golden flaxseeds	5	50 g

+ COARSELY CHOPPED KAMUT FLAKES FOR COATING (OPTIONAL)

Follow the master method on pages 34 to 37 to make the dough.

After the first two series of turns, about 1 hour into the bulk rise, add the Kamut porridge and flaxseeds gently by hand until incorporated into the dough.

Then, follow the instructions for rising, shaping, and baking on pages 38 to 41.

Roll the shaped dough in chopped Kamut flakes to coat. Place in the baskets, flake side-down seam-side up, for the final rise.

Yield: Two loaves

FARRO PORRIDGE–HAZELNUT

Farro is another ancient grain that is much higher in protein than modern wheat. Cooking the flakes yields a nutty, flavorful porridge. Toasted hazelnuts add a rich note.

FLOUR	BAKER'S %	WEIGHT
High-extraction wheat flour	50	500 g
Medium-strong wheat flour	50	500 g
WHEAT GERM	7	70 g
WATER	75	750 g
LEAVEN	15	150 g
FINE SEA SALT	2.5	25 g

ADDITIONS

Cooked farro porridge (see page 168), cooled	50	500 g
Hazelnuts, toasted, coarsely chopped (optional)	20	200 g
Hazelnut oil (optional)	5	50 g

+ FARRO FLAKES FOR COATING (OPTIONAL)

Follow the master method on pages 34 to 37 to make the dough.

After the first two series of turns, about 1 hour into the bulk rise, add the farro porridge, hazelnuts, and hazelnut oil gently by hand until incorporated into the dough.

Then, follow the instructions for rising, shaping, and baking on pages 38 to 41.

Roll the shaped dough in farro flakes to coat. Place in the baskets, flake-side down seam-side up, for the final rise.

Yield: Two loaves

OAT PORRIDGE

Rolled oats seemed the most straightforward place to begin exploring the idea of porridge-style breads. It was the first one we tried before moving on to seemingly more interesting ideas. But the rich, sweet flavor of the oats, coupled with the exceptionally moist, custardy crumb imparted by the cooked grain, have made this one of our signature breads.

FLOUR	BAKER'S %	WEIGHT
High-extraction wheat flour	50	500 g
Medium-strong wheat flour	50	500 g
WHEAT GERM	7	70 g
WATER	75	750 g
LEAVEN	15	150 g
FINE SEA SALT	2.5	25 g

ADDITIONS

Cooked oat porridge, cooled (see page 168)	50	500 g
Almonds, toasted and coarsely chopped (optional)	20	200 g
Almond oil (optional)	5	50 g

+ COARSELY CHOPPED OAT FLAKES (ROLLED OATS) FOR COATING (OPTIONAL)

Follow the master method on pages 34 to 37 to make the dough.

After the first two series of turns, about 1 hour into the bulk rise, add the oat porridge, almonds, and almond oil gently by hand until incorporated into the dough.

Then, follow the instructions for rising, shaping, and baking on pages 38 to 41.

Roll the dough in chopped oat flakes to coat. Place in the baskets, flake-side down seam-side up, for the final rise.

Yield: Two loaves

BARLEY PORRIDGE–FLAXSEED

Barley, one of oldest domesticated grains on the planet, has been used to make beer and bread since Egyptian times. While barley does contain a small amount of gluten, barley flour is not well suited to making open-textured hearth loaves. When cooked into a porridge that is high in natural gums, similar to oat and rye porridge, barley lends a custardlike texture to the bread.

FLOUR	BAKER'S %	WEIGHT
High-extraction wheat flour	50	500 g
Medium-strong wheat flour	50	500 g
WHEAT GERM	7	70 g
WATER	75	750 g
LEAVEN	15	150 g
FINE SEA SALT	2.5	25 g

PORRIDGE		
Cooked barley flake porridge (see page 168), with flaxseeds added near end of cooking, cooled	50	500 g
Golden or brown flaxseeds	5	50 g

+ COARSELY CHOPPED BARLEY FLAKES FOR COATING (OPTIONAL)

Follow the master method on pages 34 to 37 to make the dough.

After the first two series of turns, about 1 hour into the bulk rise, add the barley flake porridge and soaked flaxseeds gently by hand until incorporated into the dough.

Then follow the instructions for rising, shaping, and baking on pages 38 to 41.

Roll the dough in chopped barley flakes to coat. Place in the baskets, flake-side down seam-side up, for the final rise.

Yield: Two loaves

CRACKED CORN PORRIDGE

I've been using cooked corn polenta to flavor doughs since my early days baking in Point Reyes. Looking to use heirloom varieties of corn in a related way was the natural progression. While all the varieties we made bread with—including red, blue, purple, yellow, and orange—tasted of corn, there was certainly a notable range of flavors, with some varieties tending toward sweet and others possessing a subtle minerality.

Nixtamalized corn, which has been cooked in an alkaline solution in a ritual process used since Aztec and Mayan times, increases the nutritional value by adding certain essential vitamins and minerals and making them easier for humans to absorb. Nixtamalizing corn is the first step of preparing corn to be ground for masa, the corn-paste dough used to make tortillas, tamales, and many other Latin American staple foods.

Nixtamalizing heirloom corn for use in breads of this sort is a worthwhile endeavor, as it also intensifies the corn flavor. Nixtamalized "wet" corn mash can often be found ready-made in Latin markets. To do it yourself, the process involves boiling corn kernels for a few minutes in the alkaline water solution, letting them rest overnight in the cooking liquid, and then draining and rinsing the grain well.

To make the breads without this treatment, use a more straightforward corn porridge: Crack the corn in a powerful blender or food processor and soak overnight in water. The next day, cook the corn slowly and thoroughly until a soft corn mash is achieved. Then cool and add to the dough as with the other grain porridges.

PORRIDGE	BAKER'S %	WEIGHT
Whole-kernel dried corn, coarsely cracked (see page 170), cooked into porridge (see page 168), cooled	50	500 g
FLOUR		
High-extraction wheat flour	50	500 g
Medium-strong wheat flour	50	500 g
WHEAT GERM	7	70 g
WATER	75	750 g
LEAVEN	15	150 g
FINE SEA SALT	2.5	25 g

+ MEDIUM-FINE CRACKED CORN FOR COATING (OPTIONAL)

Follow the master method on pages 34 to 37 to make the dough.

After the first two series of turns, about 1 hour into the bulk rise, add the corn porridge gently by hand until incorporated into the dough.

Then follow the instructions for rising, shaping, and baking the loaves on pages 38 to 41.

Roll the dough in the cracked corn to coat. Place in the baskets, corn-side down seam-side up, for the final rise.

Yield: Two loaves

BROWN RICE PORRIDGE

When I began apprenticing with Richard Bourdon at his bakery in the Berkshire mountains, one of my first daily jobs was to rinse the organic brown rice three times carefully before setting it to cook long and slow in the big steam kettle we used for this task. Richard had devised a bread suited to the macrobiotic diet principles of the Kushi Institute in Becket, Massachusetts. He was motivated to create the loaf in order to counter a long-held belief within the macrobiotic movement that bread was not good for the human digestive system.

Richard's solution was to combine well-cooked whole-grain rice with a highly hydrated whole-wheat dough and let the loaves fully ferment with natural leaven to make the nutrients contained within the finished bread readily available for digestion. This incentive has only grown stronger over time and still drives our approach to whole-grain breads. Bourdon's brown rice bread is both forebear and inspiration for this bread and the other porridge breads presented here.

When preparing brown rice porridge, first rinse the rice three times before cooking to remove excess starch.

FLOUR	BAKER'S %	WEIGHT
High-extraction wheat flour	50	500 g
Medium-strong wheat flour	50	500 g
WHEAT GERM	7	70 g
WATER	85	850 g
LEAVEN	15	150 g
FINE SEA SALT	2.5	25 g
ADDITIONS		
Cooked brown rice, cooled	70	700 g

Follow the master method on pages 34 to 37 to make the dough.

After the first two series of turns, about 1 hour into the bulk rise, add the brown rice gently by hand until incorporated into the dough.

Then, follow the instructions for rising, shaping, and baking on pages 38 to 41.

Yield: Two loaves

KOJI PORRIDGE

Koji is the traditional Japanese food culture of rice inoculated with *Aspergillus oryzae* mold. It has been used for more than two thousand years to make miso, sake, soy sauce, *amazake*, pickles, and many other umami-rich foods that form the backbone of Japanese cuisine. Cortney Burns, is our co-chef (with Nick Balla) and director of special projects at Bar Tartine, where I bake bread daily in the test kitchen and for the restaurant. Cortney's latest project at the time of this writing was making koji rice in-house, preparing for a collaborative dinner we were hosting with a family that has been making koji in rural Japan since 1689, and Sonoko Sakai, an educator who works to preserve traditional Japanese food culture.

Since my early macrobiotic days working with Richard Bourdon in the Berkshires, I have been fond of *amazake*, a naturally sweet rice porridge we picked up regularly at the local food coop that is made with koji rice. Cortney was planning to make an amazake rice pudding as one of the desserts on the special menu, so we had some surplus koji rice on hand. Of course, I was inspired to make a porridge bread with this sweet addition. The pungent, sweet koji rice is a perfect complement to the slightly tart porridge-bread base dough. It's one of our favorite breads and was a hit the night of the dinner, when we served griddled slices spread with cultured butter and topped with shavings of Nick's house-cured mullet roe. One thing to keep in mind is that this bread has a significant amount of natural sugar so the crust colors much more quickly than other porridge breads. Adjust the oven temperature down by 10 to 15 percent so the bread can fully bake before burning. Dried koji rice in packages can be found in Japanese food markets and most natural food stores, or mail-ordered. Once you have the koji rice, cook as you would any typical porridge, until tender but without excess moisture.

FLOUR	BAKER'S %	WEIGHT
High-extraction wheat flour	50	500 g
Medium-strong wheat flour	50	500 g
WHEAT GERM	7	70 g
WATER	85	850 g
LEAVEN	15	150 g
FINE SEA SALT	2.5	25 g
ADDITIONS		
Koji rice porridge (see above and page 168), cooled	50	500 g

Follow the master method for porridge breads on pages 168 to 169 to make the dough.

After the first two series of turns, about 1 hour into the bulk rise, fold in the koji rice porridge gently by hand until fully incorporated.

Then, follow the instructions for rising, shaping, and baking on pages 38 to 41.

Yield: Two loaves

TOASTED MILLET PORRIDGE

Millet porridge has been eaten for thousands of years as a staple food in Africa, Asia, and India. Millet has no gluten, but in western India is traditionally used to make roti flatbreads. Here, the millet is toasted to intensify its sweet, grassy flavor and then cooked into a porridge and added to the dough.

	BAKER'S %	WEIGHT
Millet	15	150 g
FLOUR		
High-extraction wheat flour	50	500 g
Medium-strong wheat flour	50	500 g
WHEAT GERM	7	70 g
WATER	75	750 g
LEAVEN	15	150 g
FINE SEA SALT	2.5	25 g

+ RAW MILLET FOR COATING (OPTIONAL)

Preheat the oven to 350°F/180°C. Spread the millet on a baking sheet and toast until browned and aromatic, about 20 minutes. Transfer to a bowl, add 450 ml/2 cups cold water and let soak overnight. The following day, transfer the millet and soaking liquid to a medium saucepan. Bring to a boil over high heat, then reduce the heat so the water is simmering, cover, and simmer for 30 to 40 minutes, until the millet has absorbed all of the cooking liquid. Remove from the heat and let stand 10 minutes, then fluff with a fork, transfer to a baking sheet and let cool completely.

Follow the master method on pages 34 to 37 to make the dough.

After the first two series of turns, about 1 hour into the bulk rise, add the cooked, cooled millet porridge gently by hand until incorporated into the dough.

Then, follow the instructions for rising, shaping, and baking on pages 38 to 41.

Roll the dough in raw millet to coat. Place in the baskets, millet-side down seam-side up, for the final rise.

Yield: Two loaves

FERMENTED OAT

To make this bread, steel-cut oats are first coarsely cracked in a powerful blender or food processor. Next, following traditional methods described by Sandor Katz in his book *The Art of Fermentation*, the oats are soaked in water with a teaspoon of yogurt or natural leaven overnight before cooking, a means of inoculating grains with beneficial fermentation cultures to make them more digestible while also increasing nutrient density and protecting against contamination from pathogenic bacteria. Custom became catalyst as the technique gave rise to many of the bread recipes in this book.

FLOUR	BAKER'S %	WEIGHT
High-extraction wheat flour	50	500 g
Medium-strong wheat flour	50	500 g
WHEAT GERM	7	70 g
WATER	75	750 g
LEAVEN	15	150 g
FINE SEA SALT	2.5	25 g

ADDITIONS

Cracked whole oat groats, fermented overnight (see pages 168 to 169) or up to 3 days	50	500 g

+ COARSELY GROUND OAT FLAKES FOR COATING (OPTIONAL)

Follow the master method on pages 34 to 37 to make the dough, also using the master method for cracked- and flaked-grain breads (pages 170 to 171).

After the first two series of turns, about 1 hour into the bulk rise, add the cracked whole oat groats gently by hand until incorporated into the dough.

Then, follow the instructions for rising, shaping, and baking on pages 38 to 41.

Roll the dough in oat flakes. Place in the baskets, flake-side down seam-side up, for the final rise.

Yield: Two loaves

DOUBLE-FERMENTED PUMPERNICKEL

The first time I tasted true traditional Danish pumpernickel bread was at Richard Bourdon's Berkshire Mountain Bakery. It was not a bread he made often, but while I was apprenticing he wanted to show me how the old-style pumpernickel was made. Across the Midwest to the East Coast of the United States, the very dark rye bread tradition that was brought over by emigrants from Central, Eastern, and Northern Europe has largely turned to a soft pan loaf made mostly of white-wheat flour with a small portion of sour rye, often colored with caramel color and/or dark molasses.

The traditional Danish style is made with a larger portion of whole-grain rye berries in relation to whole-grain rye or whole-wheat flour. The sprouted Rene's Rye (page 140) shares some characteristics with this type of bread, but with many of the components and techniques changed. The Danish pumpernickel is fermented with natural sour rye starter and baked in sealed birch box frames in a very low oven for 13 to 15 hours. The resulting bread is very dark, heavy, and dense and naturally sweet from the thorough caramelization of the sugars in the grain during the long bake. It's a great bread, but not one that I would eat on a regular basis, as it tends to either sit heavy in the stomach or find its way out unceremoniously.

My goal in reimagining this bread was to find a way to add a large portion of whole-grain rye to the dough while retaining our favored open texture and digestibility. The addition of a small amount of blackstrap molasses complements the sour rye and shifts the flavor toward more traditional pumpernickel. Coarse cracked rye berries are first soaked and fermented overnight (or up to 3 days) then added at a ratio of 50 percent to 100 percent flour in the dough.

FLOUR	BAKER'S %	WEIGHT
High-extraction wheat flour	50	500 g
Medium-strong bread flour	50	500 g
WHEAT GERM	7	70 g
WET ADDITIONS		
Blackstrap molasses	5	50 g
WATER	75	750 g
LEAVEN	15	150 g
FINE SEA SALT	2.5	25 g
DRY ADDITIONS		
Cracked rye berries, fermented overnight or up to 3 days	50	500 g

+ RYE BRAN FOR COATING (OPTIONAL)

Follow the master method on pages 34 to 37 to make the dough, also using the master method for cracked- and flaked-grain breads (pages 170 to 171), and adding the molasses at the same time as the water and leaven.

After the first two series of turns, about 1 hour into the bulk rise, add the cracked rye berries gently by hand until incorporated into the dough.

Then, follow the instructions for rising, shaping, and baking on pages 38 to 41. Roll the dough in rye bran to coat. Place in the baskets, bran-side seam-side up, for the final rise.

Yield: Two loaves

FRANCE

Lionel Poilâne famously restored the *gros pain complet* of his father's generation from obscurity in France, putting it back on tables around the world, the denouement of a decades-long campaign to preserve and promote the *pain au levain* tradition of natural-leavened bread that had been supplanted by industrialized bread production beginning in the 1950s. By the '80s, traditional country breads had become stylish again as Parisians embraced rustic breads. Typically made with high-extraction flours, these loaves were basically a light whole grain with much of the coarse bran removed.

Poilâne may be the most renowned, but there were other artisans making distinctive, natural leavened country breads at the same time in Paris, including Lionel's brother Max Poilâne, Basil Kamir of Le Moulin de la Vierge,

natural leavened breads into the American market during the natural foods movement of the 1960s.

The Lima bakery in Ghent, Belgium, was founded in 1963 by Omer Gevaert as part of Lima, a macrobiotic natural foods company that specialized in those early years in the import of traditional Japanese fermented soy foods. The company was named after Lima Ohsawa, wife of George Ohsawa, founder of the macrobiotic movement, a philosophy of good health based in part on eating a balanced diet of Japanese whole foods. The legendary bread produced at Lima was based on the tradition of French natural-leaven country breads but was more *pain integral* than *pain complet*. The bread was called *desem*, meaning (natural) "leaven" in Flemish, and more emphasis was placed on the bread's nutritive value and digestibility than other aesthetic qualities. Yet, for many, this was the first taste of whole-grain natural-leavened bread, and the flavor was a revelation. There was dogma surrounding Lima's bread, with a mystical air lent to the unseen forces of wild fermentation and the entire breadmaking process.

Many of the earliest umami-rich Japanese foods introduced into the Western diet can be traced back to the macrobiotics movement of the 1960s: Fermented nut and grain miso, shoyu, seaweed, Japanese-style pickles, amazake, and koji were all introduced and began to be produced in California and Massachusetts (Boston being the center of macrobiotics on the East Coast) at that time. While macrobiotics gained its share of followers during the natural foods movement

Bridge over the Seine

Bernard Ganachaud, and Jean-Luc Poujauran. These French bakers inspired a parallel movement among a handful of Americans who had traveled to France to learn. In the mid-'80s, The Acme Bread Company on the West Coast and Bread Alone and Rock Hill Bake-house on the East Coast were founded; naturally leavened bread began to get a foothold here. In 1987, in an article for the *New York Times*, Florence Fabricant wrote about the growing popularity of hearth-baked country breads in the United States, linking it to the "phenomenal increase in American sophistica-tion in wine and cheese" happening around the same time.

In the same story, Fabricant also notes the earlier introduction of

method he developed before anything scientific was understood about the cellular workings of natural-leavened bread.

Dr. Herman Lerner first tasted Lima's bread in the early '70s. A physician interested in natural whole foods and health, he was struck by its depth of flavor. He traveled to Belgium to learn the breadmaking process from Omer Geveart, and founded Baldwin Hill Bakery, modeled on Lima, near Boston in 1975. This was the beginning of whole-grain natural-leavened bread in America. The desem breads of Baldwin Hill later inspired Laurel Robertson to feature the bread in Laurel's *Kitchen Bread Book*, a cherished classic of the natural foods movement.

Around the same time, Patrick LePort, a young Parisian, was eating a vegetarian diet, following the macrobiotic principles of George Ohsawa, and earning his black belt in aikido. Patrick, too, was inspired by Lima bread. In Paris, he met like-minded

View from the TGV between Paris and Brittany

in America in the '60s, Ohsawa had lived in Paris for many years, promoting his philosophy to the French before then. In the '50s, every French meal was squarely built around bread. The natural-leavened bread created at Lima fit into the macrobiotic diet and presumably helped the French warm to Ohsawa's philosophy.

At Lima, Omer Geveart's breads achieved a following within the natural food and macrobiotic communities, who praised both the bread's nutritive qualities and the method by which it was made. True desem bread, according to the writings of Geveart, was to be made with 100 percent organic whole wheat, freshly stone-milled. The water used was *eau de source*— clear mountain spring water— and the bread was baked in a wood-fired oven, as the burning wood removed from the baking chamber oxidizing gases thought to diminish nutrients in the bread.

Geveart stipulated that the leaven be prepared at dawn in

macrobiotic disciples on their way to Amsterdam to open a bakery and joined their fortuitous adventure. With no formal baking training and few to learn from as traditional baking had not yet made its roaring return, Patrick taught himself to make natural-leavened whole-grain bread. The bakery in Amsterdam was called Manna; it's where Richard Bourdon learned the basic philosophy he would later build on at his Massachusetts bakery in the Berkshire mountains where I apprenticed years later. Richard and Patrick didn't overlap at Manna; by the time Richard had become the chief baker there, Patrick had already settled in the Bauges mountain range in France where he built a massive double-deck wood-fired oven and was using direct-source mountain spring water and fresh-milled whole-grain flour to make his loaves. Something remarkable was

Françoise and Patrick

a misty pine forest when dew was covering the ground. Whole-grain wheat berries were washed and soaked in spring water, then crushed to a paste once they had softened. This paste is buried in fresh whole-grain flour and left for at least a full day's time at cool ambient temperature. During this time enzymatic activity begins, as does the wild fermentation. With desem leaven maintenance, the early stages of feeding are dry and cool, with the notion of stressing the leaven to make it stronger. These cool, dry stages produce a very sweet-smelling starter. Later stages are fed warmer and with increased hydration to encourage wild yeast and favor lactic bacterial fermentation to yield a milder acid flavor in the dough. Gevaert's method was essentially creating a multistage sequence to favor different microorganisms at different parts of the process, a

followed by a year working with Dave Miller to help open his bakery a few hours north of San Francisco. I traveled to France to learn from Patrick and his good friend Daniel Collin. The whole-grain thread was constant with all the bakers I learned from. Miller was, and still is, the only one who mills his own flour daily, but each baker specialized in making whole-grain breads. All the approaches differed but the principles were the same: organic or biodynamic grain, ample hydration, slow and gentle mixing, and long rising time using wild leaven.

While working with Patrick on our first visit to the Savoie in 1994, Liz and I planned our return to the States and sent a few letters of query, one to a cattle ranch in Marshall, California, near Tomales Bay just north of San Francisco where Alan Scott lived as a caretaker

Patrick's four Voisin

happening in the French Alps: Patrick was making striking Savoyarde country loaves with a singular savor and tender, open crumb that stood out from the rest. Bags of his massive miche were shipped weekly to Restaurant Paul Bocuse in Lyon. Word of Patrick's radical bread reached Manna while Bourdon was there, and he arranged to work with Patrick at his bakeshop in the Alps during his next vacation.

Patrick introduced Richard to "slack" doughs, which boasted unusually high hydration and lively natural fermentation. Patrick liked the challenge of making impossible bread, or, as Richard likes to say, "making water stand up." The flavors and texture of the bread were vastly improved by increasing hydration. This was especially true regarding whole-grain breads. When Richard returned to Manna after apprenticing with Patrick, the doughs began trending toward higher hydration. With a higher liquid-to-flour ratio, the starches could be more completely gelatinized during the final baking, rendering nutrients easier to assimilate and the bread more digestible. Bourdon brought this conviction to the States, and it's the first thing I learned from him as his apprentice. This high hydration principle still constitutes half the core of the Tartine approach to bread, the other half being natural leaven. Separate the two, and the bread we make is not possible. After working with Richard Bourdon for a couple of years,

in a sprawling farmhouse. I didn't know much about Alan except that at the time he was the North American authority on building wood-fired masonry ovens, and that he'd let you live on the ranch if there was room and you could help out around the property. We had little money and no clear plan, so this seemed like a good option.

Getting to know Alan the first few weeks, we learned he had built his first wood-fired oven in order to bake a true desem bread in the tradition of the Lima bakery for his friend Laurel Robertson at the ZenCenter nearby. There was a small oven in the yard just off the kitchen that I was welcome to use. This was the beginning of Tartine bread.

Patrick's *pain au levain*

CRISP-BREADS

Crispbreads are thin, baked, and dehydrated bread doughs that have a crackerlike texture. Doughs destined to become crispbreads are mixed with a lower hydration (50 to 60 percent) so that they can be rolled out very thinly: about as thick as a sheet of medium-weight paper. The typical Tartine bread dough has 85 percent hydration, which is near impossible to roll thin without sticking. Developing recipes for these crispbreads is straightforward, you simply decrease the amount of hydration in the Tartine master bread dough recipes.

The less conventional sprouted pan loaves require a different approach when converting to crispbreads. I love the flavor of Rene's Rye and thought it would make a tasty crispbread. But the whole rye berries and some of the larger seeds made it impossible to roll thinly enough. So I deconstructed the bread dough and reconstructed it as a crispbread, mixing the dough with a lower hydration, roughly chopping the sprouted rye berries, and reserving the seeds as topping for the crackers instead of incorporating them into the dough.

MASTER METHOD
FOR CRISPBREADS

In order to maintain a reasonable yield of ten crispbreads, we've scaled the flour in all these recipes to 500 grams rather than 1 kilogram.

Mix the dough using the master method on pages 34 to 37 with the reduced hydration indication in each crispbread recipe. Let ferment overnight, covered, in the refrigerator. The next day, divide the dough into small pieces, each about 50 grams, and shape into rounds. Let rest for 10 to 15 minutes.

To make by hand: Coat the work surface (I prefer wood), with whole-grain wheat or rye flour (or bran) and place one dough piece on the floured surface. Coat the top of the dough with more flour and, using a French rolling pin, roll the dough into loose rounds as thin as possible. Flip, coating with more flour as

needed to prevent sticking, and continue rolling until you have a piece of dough that is evenly thin.

Carefully transfer the dough to a parchment-lined baking sheet. Brush the crispbread with water and sprinkle with toppings, pressing lightly to adhere them to the dough. Bake at 425°F/220°C until golden brown, 10 to 15 minutes.

Keep a close eye on the color. When the dough is rolled so thinly, once it starts to color it browns quickly. Let cool slightly, then carefully remove from the baking sheet and transfer to a cooling rack. Repeat with the remaining pieces of dough. At this point the crispbreads are baked, but they still need to be further dehydrated and crisped.

Reduce the oven temperature to 200°F/95°C. When the oven has cooled to that temperature, place the crispbreads in the oven, directly on the oven racks.

To allow moisture to escape, leave the oven door slightly cracked (use the handle of a wooden spoon to keep it ajar), and bake 10 to 15 minutes longer, until the crispbreads are thoroughly dehydrated; they should not darken in color.

Carefully remove from the oven and transfer to a cooling rack. Once cool, break into large pieces or transfer whole to an airtight container right away so they stay crisp; they will keep for a week stored properly and can be recrisped by heating again in a moderate oven (300°F/150°C) for 10 to 12 minutes.

To make with a pasta machine: Alternatively, crispbread dough can be rolled through a pasta machine. All of the doughs in this chapter, with the exception of René-Style Crispbreads (page 216), which contains sprouted grains and therefore cannot be rolled thinly enough, are well-suited to the pasta-machine technique.

After your crispbread dough has fermented overnight, pull it out of the refrigerator. Lightly flour the top and cut into two 250-gram pieces.

Flour your work surface and the dough. With a rolling pin, roll one piece of dough just thin enough so it will fit through the widest setting on your pasta machine. Flour the dough well, then feed it through the machine. Repeat this step, reducing the opening of the rollers a notch with each pass until you've reached

CRISPBREADS

the Number 1 setting on the pasta machine, flouring the dough each time as necessary to prevent sticking.

As the dough gets thinner, use the backs of your hands to guide the dough through the rollers to help prevent tears. If at any time you feel your dough is too long to manage, cut it in half and roll both pieces separately.

Transfer the dough to a well-floured work surface. Follow the steps for baking as described for the rolling pin method. Repeat the process with the remaining piece of dough.

MASTER METHOD
FOR FILLED CRISPBREADS

There is a traditional pasta-making technique in which herbs or other aromatics are rolled between very thin sheets of dough so the pasta becomes translucent and the herb pattern decorative. Since we began to use the pasta machine to make many of our crispbreads extra-thin, the obvious notion to fill the crispbread with decorative flavoring led to an eleventh-hour round of experimentation. We've had great luck experimenting with filled crackers. Soft herbs and flowers such as tarragon, chives and their blossoms, borage, and marigold petals can be sandwiched between thin layers of dough, giving the finished crackers a stained-glass look; fresh nettles also work well, as well as paper-thin slices of raw beet, celery root, and carrot. Slivered almonds are nice, too. Sandwiching flavorings into the crispbread creates tiny bubbles across the surface of the dough that, once baked, add an extra-crisp character. In pasta making, the bubbles are a flaw; with crispbreads they are a welcome surprise.

To make filled crispbreads, after the final pass through the pasta machine, transfer the dough to a well-floured work surface. Roughly mark the center of your dough and, with a pastry brush, brush one half lightly with water. Lay the filling of your choice on the moistened half of the dough in a single layer, arranging it artfully, then fold the dough, encasing the filling, and pat well so that the two pieces of dough adhere to one another.

Flour the dough well, then run it through the pasta machine again, beginning at the Number 4 or 5 setting and continuing until you've passed the dough through the Number 1 or 2 setting (the settings depend on the thickness of the filling).

Transfer the dough to a floured surface and cut each crispbread into the desired shape, transfer to a parchment-lined baking sheet, and brush with melted butter. Bake at 425°F/220°C for 10 to 15 minutes, until golden brown. Remove from the oven.

Reduce the oven temperature to 200°F/95°C. When the oven has cooled, remove the crispbreads from the baking sheets and return them to the oven, placing them directly on the oven racks. To allow moisture to escape, leave the oven door slightly cracked (use the handle of a wooden spoon to keep it ajar), and bake 10 to 15 minutes longer, until the crispbreads are thoroughly dehydrated. They should not have darkened in color.

Carefully remove from the oven and transfer to a cooling rack. Once cool, break into large pieces or transfer whole to an airtight container right away so they stay crisp; they will keep for a week stored properly and can be recrisped by heating again in a moderate oven (300°F/150°C) for 10 to 12 minutes.

WHEAT-SPELT CRISPBREADS WITH SESAME & FENNEL SEEDS

My dear friend, Kille Enna, first taught me her technique to make crispbreads using flour grown and milled fresh on Camilla Plum's farm outside of Copenhagen. After I returned home, we started making this basic seeded crispbread to accompany early spring pea and fava bean dishes served with fresh farmer's cheese at Bar Tartine.

FLOUR	BAKER'S %	WEIGHT
High-extraction whole-grain spelt flour	50	142 g
Medium-strong wheat flour	30	85 g
High-extraction whole-grain wheat flour	20	57 g
WHEAT GERM	7	20 g
FINE SEA SALT	2.5	7 g

WATER	50	142 g
LEAVEN	15	42 g

ADDITIONS

Sesame seeds		300 g
Fennel seeds		100 g

TOPPINGS

Flaky sea salt, such as Maldon		100 g

Follow the master method on pages 34 to 37 to make the dough, adjusted for crispbreads as on page 206, adding the wheat germ and fine sea salt to the flour before combining with the water-leaven mixture. Let ferment overnight, covered, in the refrigerator.

In a small bowl, combine the sesame and fennel seeds. Portion the dough, let rest, and then roll out, transfer to the baking sheets, and lightly brush with water as described on pages 206. Top each piece with some of the seed mixture, pressing lightly so the seeds adhere to the dough. Season each piece with crushed salt.

Bake as instructed on page 206.

Yield: Ten crispbreads

WHEAT-RYE CRISPBREADS WITH CARAWAY

My friend Stefan Berg, who runs Valhalla Bageriet in Stockholm, makes the excellent bread served at restaurant Mathias Dahlgren. When Stefan worked with us at Tartine during a visit in 2012, I asked him to teach us the Swedish technique for making traditional knäckebröd, or crispbreads, a staple food of Scandinavia for over a thousand years.

FLOUR	BAKER'S %	WEIGHT
High-extraction whole-grain wheat flour	40	113 g
Medium-strong wheat flour	30	85 g
Whole-grain dark rye flour	20	57 g
Whole-grain wheat flour	10	28 g
WHEAT GERM	7	20 g
FINE SEA SALT	2.5	7 g

ADDITIONS		
Caraway seeds, toasted and coarsely ground	3	8 g

WATER	50	140 g
LEAVEN	15	42 g

TOPPINGS		
Flaky sea salt, such as Maldon		100 g
Caraway seeds, toasted and coarsely ground		100 g

Follow the master method on pages 34 to 37 to make the dough, adjusted for crispbreads as on page 206, adding the wheat germ, fine sea salt, and ground caraway seeds to the flour before combining with the water-leaven mixture. Let ferment overnight, covered, in the refrigerator.

Portion the dough, let rest, and then roll out, transfer to the baking sheets, and brush with water as described on pages 206. Top each piece with some of the flaky sea salt and crushed caraway seeds, pressing lightly so they adhere to the dough.

Bake as instructed on page 206.

Yield: Ten crispbreads

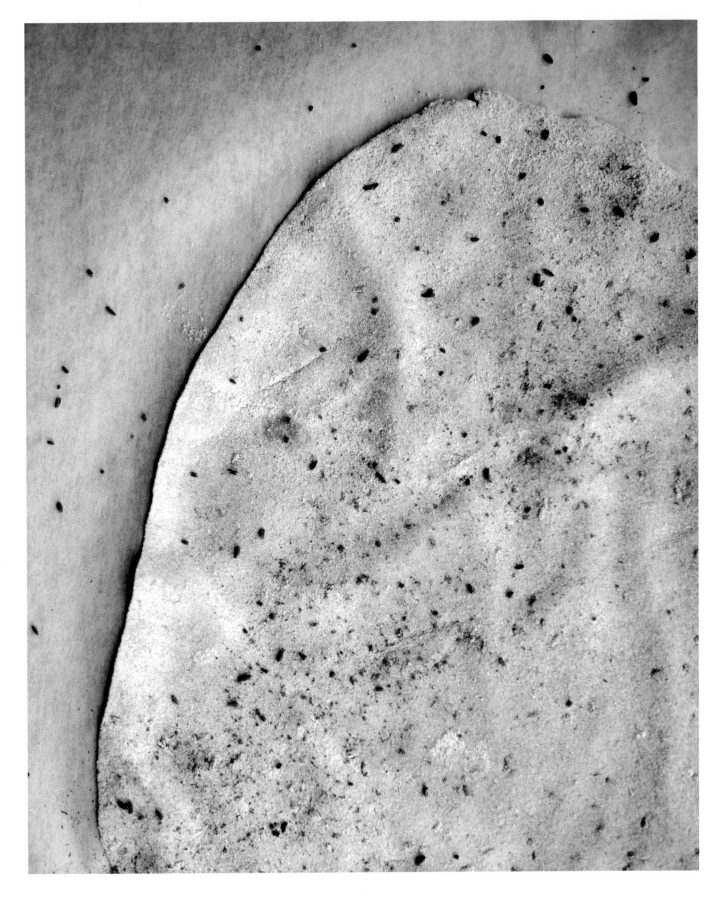

CRISPBREADS

RENÉ-STYLE CRISPBREADS

At the bakery we continue to explore new iterations of René Rye (page 140), which is loaded with seeds and sprouted grains. For the crispbread, we deconstruct the rye bread dough, reducing the hydration and using the larger seeds as a topping (instead of in the dough) so it can still be rolled very thin.

FLOUR	BAKER'S %	WEIGHT
High-extraction whole-grain spelt flour	80	102 g
Whole-grain dark rye flour	20	26 g
GROUND FLAXSEEDS	15	20 g
FINE SEA SALT	4	5 g
WET ADDITIONS		
Buttermilk	36	46 g
Dark beer	27	35 g
Malt syrup	4	5 g
WATER	25	32 g
LEAVEN	62	80 g

DRY ADDITIONS		
Sprouted rye berries, coarsely chopped	105	135 g
TOPPINGS		
Sunflower seeds		250 g
Pumpkin seeds		250 g
Sesame seeds		100 g
Flaxseeds		100 g
Flaky sea salt, such as Maldon		100 g

Follow the master method on pages 34 to 37 to make the dough, adjusted for crispbreads as on page 206, adding the ground flaxseed and fine sea salt to the flour and adding the buttermilk, beer, and malt syrup at the same time you add the water to the water-leaven mixture. Let rest 30 minutes, then stir in the coarsely chopped sprouted rye. Let ferment overnight, covered, in the refrigerator.

In a small bowl, combine the sunflower, pumpkin seeds, sesame seeds, and whole flaxseeds. Portion the dough, let rest, and then roll out, transfer to the baking sheets, and brush with water as described on page 206. Top each piece with some of the seed mixture, pressing lightly so the seeds adhere to the dough. Season each piece with flaky sea salt.

Bake as instructed on page 206.

Yield: Ten crispbreads

CRISPBREADS

BUCKWHEAT-NORI CRISPBREADS

This crispbread has crushed toasted nori mixed into the dough and is topped with black, or unhulled, sesame seeds. You can also sandwich sheets of the dried seaweed between layers of a lighter-colored crispbread dough, such as the Kamut (see page 224), then passing the dough through the rollers of a pasta machine (see Master Method for Filled Crispbreads, page 210). The dough sheets crack as the dough is rolled thin, creating a striated geometric pattern and revealing the nori within.

FLOUR	BAKER'S %	WEIGHT
Whole-grain buckwheat flour	40	105 g
High-extraction whole-grain wheat flour	30	79 g
Medium-strong bread flour	30	79 g
WHEAT GERM	7	20 g
FINE SEA SALT	2.5	7 g

ADDITIONS		
Nori, toasted and coarsely ground	3	8 g

WATER	60	158 g
LEAVEN	15	40 g

TOPPINGS		
Black sesame seeds		300 g
Flaky sea salt, such as Maldon		100 g

Follow the master method on pages 34 to 37 to make the dough, adjusted for crispbreads as on page 206, adding the wheat germ, fine sea salt, and nori to the flour before combining with the water-leaven mixture. Let ferment overnight, covered, in the refrigerator.

Portion the dough, let rest, and then roll out, transfer to the baking sheets, and brush with water as described on page 206. Top each piece with sesame seeds, pressing lightly so the seeds adhere to the dough. Season each piece with flaky sea salt.

Bake as instructed on page 206.

Yield: Ten crispbreads

CRISPBREADS

OATMEAL-PORRIDGE CRISPBREADS

One of our favorite signature breads is presented here in crispbread form. It makes an especially aromatic and delicate cracker when sandwiched with sliced almonds.

ADDITIONS	BAKER'S %	WEIGHT
Cooked oatmeal porridge (see page 168), cooled	50	127 g
WATER	20	51 g
LEAVEN	15	38 g
FLOUR		
High-extraction whole-grain wheat flour	50	127 g
Medium-strong bread flour	50	127 g
WHEAT GERM	7	20 g
FINE SEA SALT	2.5	7 g

+ SLICED ALMONDS FOR FILLING (OPTIONAL)

In a large bowl, mix together the porridge, water, and leaven. Add the flour, wheat germ, and fine sea salt and mix well until incorporated. Let ferment overnight, covered, in the refrigerator.

Portion the dough, let rest, and then roll out, transferring to the baking sheets. If filling with nuts, use the pasta machine method (see page 210), then brush with melted butter.

Bake as instructed on page 206.

Yield: Ten crispbreads

CRISPBREADS

CRISPBREADS

KAMUT CRISPBREADS

Kamut flour produces the lightest golden trans-lucent color of all the crispbreads, so we use it to sandwich different herbs, edible flowers, and shaved vegetables—beets, carrots, nettles, garlic shoots, borage, bronze fennel, clover, and nasturtiums. We were thinking of Michel Bras' exquisite Gargouillou preparation, along with the epic Sardinian-style crispbread, *carta di musica,* that chef Jeremy Fox was making at Ubuntu a few years ago. This crispbread is a modest salute.

Follow the master method on pages 34 to 37 to make the dough, adjusted for crispbreads as on page 206, adding the wheat germ and fine sea salt to the flour before combining with the water-leaven mixture. Let ferment overnight, covered, in the refrigerator.

Portion the dough, let rest, and then roll out, transfer to the baking sheets. If filling, use the pasta machine method (see page 210), then brush with melted butter. Season each piece with flaky salt.

Bake as instructed on page 206.

Yield: Ten crispbreads

FLOUR	BAKER'S %	WEIGHT
Whole-grain Kamut flour	60	170 g
Medium-strong bread flour	40	113 g
WHEAT GERM	7	20 g
FINE SEA SALT	2.5	7 g
WATER	50	142 g
LEAVEN	15	45 g

+ HERBS, EDIBLE FLOWERS, AND SHAVED VEGETABLES FOR FILLING (OPTIONAL) AND FLAKY SEA SALT, SUCH AS MALDON

CRISPBREADS

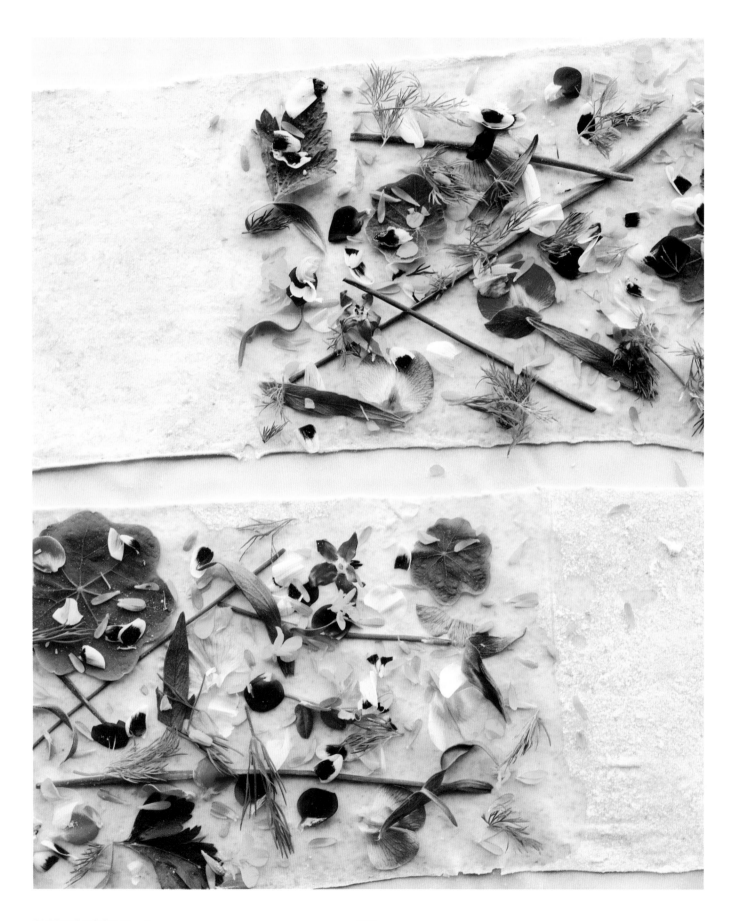

CRISPBREADS

MEXICO

I had seen photos of the house on the beach and heard tales of excellent regional meals prepared by the caretakers, Augustina and Paulie. But we were headed to the coast of the Mexican state of Guerrero for the waves. This was the first of what would become a yearly trip where our group of friends—roughly half from Brooklyn and the rest from San Francisco—converged to catch up over a week of surf and food. Typically this was the most we saw of each other until next year's visit. Of course, most of us had packed laptops or notebooks, planning to take advantage of the remote sequestration to get stuff done.

Dave Muller, my close friend and founder of Outerlands, a pioneering restaurant located a few blocks from our home break in San Francisco, makes great natural-leavened bread daily at his place. He learned some

world from scratch—my Scandinavian travels would come later. I was well into working on the manuscript for my first book, *Tartine Bread*, and aimed to write in the afternoons after surfing in the morning. The heart of that book is about building a natural leaven, and I was currently expressing my observation that the natural leaven was much less a product of place and much more a product of patterns: predictable patterns of time and temperature in the leaven's feeding schedules. In my experience, the leaven went through multiple stages when the microbiology would shift. Each stage was different and each was important, adding distinct flavor qualities throughout the cycle. That and the ingredients (the type of flour, liquid, or other additions such as fruit) would determine the character of the leaven. Place was simply that, but San Francisco's notably temperate weather is admittedly perfectly suited to maintaining a healthy leaven most of the year.

We had six days in Mexico. I figured if we mixed up a leaven as soon as we got to the house we might have a loaf of bread before we headed home. It was, after all, southern Mexico, with warm days and cool nights, much like an Indian summer in the Mission District back home. That said, Dave and I were both decidedly skeptical. Augustina made fresh tortillas daily so there was always corn masa in the kitchen. Luckily for us she had a small bag of *harina integral*, Mexican whole-wheat flour we could use to

Charring citrus, Zihuatenejo

bread techniques working with us at Tartine before he opened his own space. We traveled to Mexico together, and on the flight heading down, Dave suggested we make some bread while we were there. Honestly, the thought hadn't occurred to me but Dave was new to making bread. His tenderfoot obsession with baking was still strong—and catching, too.

Neither of us had brought starter, and we had no idea how well suited the Mexican flour would be to making our style of bread. This was the first time I would be making bread in a different part of the

phases occurs over the two-year fermentation period, changing with seasonal temperature fluctuations, pH levels, and available food sources and oxygen. This sequential pattern of wild fermentation is the key process responsible for the layered, distinctive flavors of lambic beers.

Lambic brewers are conducting a symphony of natural processes, acting as both catalysts and shepherds in an attempt to achieve the desired outcome. The notion that the pattern has a specific sequence was a revelation; there was surely something valuable in this discovery related to bread. Lambic beers typically go through at least five distinct phases of fermentation. Unlike more common styles of beer where the flavor character is

Beach bonfire, Zihuatenejo

start the leaven. This was ideal: Whole grain has more nutrients to feed the wild yeast and bacteria, so they grew more vigorously. With so little time, it was key to get the leaven kicking.

In the mid-'90s, a few years into my fascination with wild fermentation, I was introduced by a beer-loving friend to the distinguished lambic beers of Belgium. Michael Jackson, an authority on beer, described lambics as "the world's most unusual, complex, and fascinating beers" in his wholehearted endorsement of the book *Lambic* by Jean-Xavier Guinard. When Michael Jackson died in 2007, the beer world lost its chief missionary; his encyclopedic writings on beer will inform future generations.

These beers are naturally fermented over the course of about two years on average. Lambics still retain an air of mystery, and their distinct complexity is undiminished. But in the mid-'70s, extensive scientific study gave us a glimpse into the microcosms of wild yeasts and bacteria at work throughout the process of fermentation that barrel-aged lambics undergo before they are ready for drinking. The term "wild yeast" literally references the fact that they are out of the brewer's control. Throughout modern brewing history, there have been essentially two main yeasts used for making beer—the others are considered contaminants. This is where lambic is so unique. A specifically sequenced pattern of wild yeast and bacterial

mostly determined by the types of grain and hops used, lambic's complex character is shaped in large part by the wild fermentation, which changes with seasonal temperature fluctuations among other things. The origins of the lambic process and the way our bread was taking shape were closely related. Over time, the concept of sequential phases of fermentation would illuminate parts of my bread-making process that had been invisible before.

Two decades ago, when I began working with natural-leavened bread, if something

was off, and the resulting bread suffered, my first instinct was to blame things I could quantify easily—the things I could see. Oftentimes I assumed that something must have changed with the new batch of flour; maybe the gluten was not

Dave's ocean water bread

wild yeasts and bacteria get situated in the mix. Some characters that don't contribute to the desirable flavors you want dissipate and disappear quickly as the culture acidifies and matures into a healthy sourdough environment.

I continued to discard half of the starter, refreshing it with fresh flour and water early each day before paddling out to surf the point at sunrise. By day three, it started to smell like my leaven at Tartine, sweet and lactic. On day four we made pizza using the leaven, and by day five we had respectable loaves of bread on the family table for dinner.

Replicating the Tartine starter over a few days in southern Mexico using the native flour confirmed a notion when I had first smelled Patrick LePort's young leaven in Brittany a couple of years before. The

Shaping loaves

as tolerant to my bent toward high hydration and a very long rise. Yet, over the years, experience has almost always pointed in one direction, inevitably coming down to the condition of the leaven. The leaven itself is highly sensitive to temperature fluctuations and to the food that is fueling its sustained growth.

A negative turn in the bread at Tartine these days triggers a swift forensic response that starts with an algorithm. We work backward, imagining ourselves in the bucket as the living leaven. When we track the pattern of time, temperature, and food source, the problem is always solved, often in simple ways.

Tartine bread goes through a process closer to a 24-hour cycle than the 24-month cycle of lambic beer. With bread I am working with fewer dominant types of

leaven Patrick used to make his regular breads was very different from mine. It was fed on a different cycle, at different temperatures, and with different percentages of inoculating starter. But Patrick had another leaven he used for his baguettes, one he maintained specifically to promote the wild yeast activity and keep the acetic acid low, one that behaved and smelled much like my San Francisco leaven, with similar character. It was the beginning of an important realization: The character of leaven is not inherently sensitive to location. This realization was further supported by the taste and appearance of those loaves in Mexico, which were so much like Tartine bread, so far from Tartine.

wild microorganisms than the extraordinarily diverse process that produces lambic. But as much as I try to control the process on the one hand, letting the wild fermentation go through very active phases to develop depths of flavor is key to my approach. Minimal manipulation in the early stages—to allow maximum expression and transformation wrought by the microflora—is always the goal.

Back in Mexico, I mixed a batter with the whole-wheat flour and water, covered it with a kitchen cloth, and set it on the shelf. The next morning, it was already actively fermenting, but it didn't smell so great. This is normal, though. Off aromas are often present in the beginning as dozens of

Left point

PASTRY

Tartine pastries are built on classic recipes. My wife, Liz, and I were both trained in traditional European pastry and baking techniques in culinary school, but we had both grown up with whole food–leaning mothers, who served us brown rice, whole-grain bread, and lots of vegetables and tofu. When I started working with Richard Bourdon at his bakery in the Berkshire mountains, Liz worked there too. But she was more inclined to the fine calibration of the pastry arts than the rough calculation and heavy lifting of bread work. Soon after we moved to western Massachusetts, Liz started working as a pastry chef at Canyon Ranch so we could stay together while I finished my apprenticeship with Bourdon. At Canyon Ranch, Liz applied classical techniques using whole-food ingredients. Working with a nutritionist, the goal was to create desserts with balanced sweetness and lower fat content.

I've never had much of a sweet tooth, preferring cheese, coffee, or a square of dark chocolate to end my meals. During my recent culinary travels, the final courses I've enjoyed the most have been forward thinking, using ingredients typically suited more to the savory side of the kitchen and notably less sweet: sunchokes with coffee powder and passion fruit at Relae, celery root tea cake with celery seed at Isa, and the sorrel curd tarts with charred citrus rind Bo Bech made when he came to San Francisco to cook at Bar Tartine.

For the holidays at the bakery this year, we decreased the sugar in our steamed ginger pudding and added beet and espresso, slightly recalibrating one of my favorite recipes. The new recipe took me back to the time when Liz and I had just made our way from the East Coast to California. Liz was charged with making a menu of whole-food pastries using biodynamic flours milled fresh daily at Dave Miller's bakery, which we helped open.

Liz set to work, recording her recipes in a small black notebook. After we left Dave to work in the south of France, she affixed a sticker to the notebook. The singular aim proclaimed by that sticker has not changed a bit since: TRES BIEN! would do, and nothing less. I had no idea what she was up to. Soon a chocolate cake made with Kamut, mayonnaise, and vinegar appeared, along with spiced carrot cake with tofu emulsion in place of the eggs, colored and flavored with tamarind and maple. She experimented with fudgy brownies made with whole-grain rye flour, prune purée, tahini, and strong coffee. There

were pecan caramels made with *amazake*, the ancient Japanese sweet made from rice cultured with *koji*, and addictive carob cookies with ground flaxseeds and almond butter, sweetened with chopped currants. It was 1993, and what Liz was doing was definitely far-out.

We had eaten barley and hazelnut sablés at Daniel Collin's bakery in Provence during our apprenticeship there, after we settled in with the naturalists who had colonized the abandoned wine château. As a young man, Daniel had spent part of the early 1980s in Northern California teaching traditional natural-leaven French baking to a French expat named Jean Ponce. When Daniel returned to France, he brought with him an open-mindedness gained from his time in California. Making French sablés in rural Provence using organic whole-barley flour is as radical now as it was then, and Daniel opened the door for this exploration.

Tartine Book No. 3 started as a whole-grain bread book. Soon after beginning to test ideas and create recipes with the various grains, it made no sense to neglect the pastry side of our production. We have a talented team in the kitchen, and everyone wanted to participate in the research and development. It was time to crack Liz's notebook and see how these ideas tasted twenty years later.

Cookies seemed the natural place to start: The basic French sablé ratio and technique could not be more perfectly engineered. Buckwheat, oats, barley, Kamut—pretty much any good baking-quality cereal or grain would work. Fitting the right flavors and textures together with spices, aromatics, and various sweeteners was the formula that needed to be worked out. And figure it out we did—dozens of delicious variations sprang to life.

Tea cakes, too, are fairly straightforward, and it's easy enough to substitute part or, in some cases, all of the sifted white pastry or cake flour for more flavorful whole-grain varieties, as the cakes don't rely on gluten to give them strength. Whole-grain tea cakes can be heavy, though, so I applied techniques typically used to make flaky doughs or biscuits. The result is a cake with a lighter, more aerated crumb that belies the whole-grain trade-off.

Just as I've been considering sifted white flour as a sort of "flavor neutral" component that could be improved by replacing some or all of it with more flavorful, less refined grains, so too I'm considering sugar the same way. Pure white granulated sugar is used to sweeten, but I'd rather think of it as a flavoring agent; using less of it on the whole, and choosing more varied and unrefined types of sugar and other whole foods that both sweeten and flavor. So we experimented using raw wildflower honey in our lemon cream, or currants and dates in a basic tea cake. Looking at the wider world of sugars had much the same expansive effect as using the greater variety of grains on the possible flavors we could achieve.

Mexican and Central American styles of *horchata*—spiced rice milk—are abundant all over our neighborhood, and we often make refreshing batches poured over ice on hot summer days for our staff meal. The simplest version is typically made with rice, flavored with cinnamon, and sweetened with sugar. Our neighborhood *horchatas* were the inspiration, but also the point of departure for us to work new flavors into classic preparations. In recipes that called for dairy products like milk or cream, we've experimented with making and using different nut milks so we're starting out with a more flavorful building block. We culture cream and butter with lacto or kefir cultures, yielding two completely different flavor profiles.

Some of these things—like using crème fraîche in our quiche batter, a subtle detail that contributes outsized flavor—we've been doing since the beginning at Tartine. Why not, I thought, apply this approach to the rest of what we do and see if we can improve an already solid recipe, making it both tastier and more nutritious at the same time? Fresh ideas with more depth of flavor often resulted from this recasting of classic Tartine recipes, and these are the recipes I'm presenting here.

SUGAR PRIMER

There are dozens of types of granulated and syrup sugars suitable for use in making pastry. Here, I focus on the whole-food varieties that are readily available and complement the recipes well. Finding that various types of flours added fresh flavors and textures to classic Tartine preparations, we then began to swap in different, less-refined sugars following the same train of thought.

Refined white sugar is essentially a sweetener without any distinct flavor beyond the sweetness. The amber-colored organic sugar that we have used for years at Tartine is slightly less refined than the pure white type but still functions much the same way. To make *superfine* sugar, we simply grind organic sugar in a food processor.

Obviously, there were other more interesting paths to explore. Specific sugars chosen for use in the recipes here are not necessarily the only ones that can be used, but are the choices we settled on while testing—taking into consideration flavor, color, and the overall character it added. As I discovered when I began baking with flours beyond white and whole-wheat, a fascinating world of flavor exists beyond white and brown sugar.

Just choosing which honey to use in a recipe quickly reveals an astonishingly vast range and intensity of flavor and colors. **Honey** is made from flower nectar and differs in taste depending on the blossom from which the pollen is harvested. Some more savory honeys are made from buckwheat, star thistle, bor- age, and herbs such as thyme and rosemary. Floral, fruity honeys come from eucalyptus, cherry, and peach blossoms.

When a recipe calls for brown sugar—a blend of generic refined white sugar and molasses—there are more interesting options available. True **muscovado sugar** is partially refined sugar harvested from the process before all of the molasses has been separated from the sucrose. **Light muscovado** has less molasses than dark. **Dark muscovado** has a more varied and complex flavor than commercial brown sugar, and origin-specific muscovados from Mauritius, Barbados, and the Philippines, for example, can be quite distinct from each other.

Some much less refined sugars are made by pressing sugarcane juice and then reducing it by boiling and evaporation into syrup, which is then poured into cones or cakes and cools to a hard, fudgy consistency. In Southeast Asia and India, this family of sugars is called *jaggery* and is used hard, soft, and all states in between in both sweet and savory preparations. Flavors range from light caramel to dark molasses and vary regionally. The hard forms can be ground into irregular granules. In Latin America, the fudgy cones are called *piloncillo*; Mexican varieties often have a pleasant butter-scotch flavor. *Sucanat* is a similar product sourced from Costa Rica made from pure evaporated cane juice but with a caramelized flavor somewhere between light and dark jaggery.

One type of jaggery from Southeast Asia and India is made from the sap of the date palm; another from the nectar of coconut palm blossoms. The sap and nectar are reduced and ground to a typically moist granulation. Both are used to add distinct complementary flavors to tea cakes and cookies.

Maple syrup, made from the sap of maple trees, is graded; grade A is light gold and sweet, with a light maple flavor, while grade B syrup is darker, more viscous, and has a more pronounced maple flavor. Maple syrup is also available in granulated form, called **maple sugar**. Maple syrup is more common in North America, whereas birch syrup is used in Northern and Eastern Europe and Russia.

Date sugar, different from date palm sugar, is simply made from dried and ground whole dates and is the only sugar used in this book that is not water soluble. Date sugar is perfect for adding a crisp edge to palmiers and cookies, finishing tarts mixed with other aromatics and spice blends, or adding a coarse-textured whole-food sweetener to tea cakes or cookies.

CULTURED DAIRY PRIMER: SOURED CREAM AND KEFIR

Soured cream and kefir are both cultured dairy products made from milk or cream, but the cultures used to make the two are different. Many types of milks or creams are suitable for sour dairy or kefir applications; the fermentation process renders the dairy more digestible and nutrient-rich by the action of the microorganisms. There are many health benefits to cultured dairy products, which are loaded with probiotics, but I am primarily interested in the flavor benefits. A grilled cheese sandwich always tastes better when fried up with cultured butter.

Soured cream is made by inoculating the dairy with lactic bacterial cultures at specific temperatures for certain amounts of time. The culture used to sour fresh cream or milk can be a small bit from an already soured batch. **Crème fraîche** is a younger and milder (less sour) French style of soured cream. **Yogurt** is also in this same family, but typically made with milk instead of cream and found in different consistencies determined by fat percentage, depth of culturing, and straining off a portion of the liquid whey to make a thicker, richer texture. Yogurt often requires a warm inoculation to achieve proper acidification. The familiar flavor of soured cream and yogurt-style cultured dairy products ranges from mildly tart to pleasantly sharp depending on how it's made.

Kefir is made similarly, but from a wider-ranging family of bacterial cultures that also includes wild yeast strains existing in symbiosis with the bacteria. Kefir cultures are bound together in tiny cauliflower-like clusters referred to as *grains*. Kefir cultures at room temperature and does not have to be heated to start the process. The wild yeast strains, in addition to carbonating the liquid with gas, also produce a small amount of alcohol by-product. The action of the yeast flavors the kefir differently than yogurt. Kefir tends toward a bright citrus flavor with noticeable effervescence on the tongue. It can also be used to culture and carbonate water-based liquids with delicious probiotic results, but we are only using dairy kefir as a component in these recipes.

As with natural-leavened bread, the taste and texture of cultured dairy products is dependent on time, temperature, and the proper balance of bacterial and yeast cultures. All of the cultures are highly sensitive to these factors and will change with the slightest shift. So, as with natural-leavened bread, care should be taken to maintain these key factors in a consistent manner.

For the pastry recipes here that call for crème fraîche or kefir cream, the two can be used interchangeably, as they typically have a similar consistency. Crème fraîche and kefir are readily available, but they are also very simple and much less expensive to make yourself at home.

Both are cultured with lactic acid bacterial cultures, but kefir is the more biologically complex of the two, and includes many strains of wild yeasts. Kefir has a slightly more citric flavor than crème fraîche. Another distinction between the two cultured creams: crème fraîche is essentially fresh cream left out to sour naturally. But to make kefir cultured dairy, one needs to start the process with kefir starter cultures called kefir grains. Kefir grains are easily sourced, and once you begin to use them, the grains multiply each time you use them so you have extra for subsequent batches.

TO MAKE KEFIR CULTURED CREAM: Begin with fresh cream in a stainless-steel bowl or glass jar and add to it live kefir grains in a ratio of about 1 part kefir grains to 10 parts cream. Tie the kefir grains in a square of cheesecloth to make it easier to remove them later. Fill your container about two-thirds full to leave room for the gases that are produced by the wild yeasts and bacteria as the cream is culturing. Cover the bowl or jar with cheesecloth and seal it with a rubber band.

Let stand at room temperature for 24 hours, or until thickened and soured to your taste. Remove the cheesecloth sachet containing the kefir grains. If you plan to reuse the kefir grains, immediately transfer the sachet to a jar of fresh milk, since kefir grains require dairy (lactose) to live. Refrigerate and refresh with fresh milk every 7 to 10 days.

TO MAKE CRÈME FRAÎCHE: Begin with fresh heavy cream in a stainless-steel bowl or glass jar and add cultured buttermilk or yogurt in a ratio of about 1 part buttermilk or yogurt to 8 parts heavy cream. Cover the bowl or jar with cheesecloth, seal it with a rubberband, and let stand at 24 hours, or until thickened and soured to your taste. The process is exactly the same as if making kefir cream, except you will not have any kefir grains to remove. Also, you can use a portion of the crème fraîche you've made to inoculate your next batch.

Butter can be made from either soured cream or kefir cream in the traditional method, mixing in a stand mixer until the fat solids separate from the liquid whey.

TO MAKE KEFIR BUTTER OR CULTURED CREAM BUTTER: Place kefir cultured cream or crème fraîche in a stand mixer or fill a glass jar two-thirds full and fit with a tight lid. Shake the jar vigorously until the butter fat solids separate from the liquid whey. Pour into a colander set over a bowl and strain off the whey (reserve the whey for another use; it can be substituted for buttermilk). Remove the solids from the colander and immerse in ice water, squeezing the butter mass to remove any remaining whey.

CROQUANT D'AMANDES

Liz made these *bisquits* years ago when we lived next to the bakery in Point Reyes. We baked in a wood-fired oven, and twice a week we'd drive our bread and pastries to sell at the Berkeley Farmers' Market. Originally flavored with dried lavender, a holdover from our time spent baking in Provence, I wanted something less sweet and less perfumed but held on to the notion of flower petals. Here, the tart crimson hibiscus blossoms sharpen the flavor of these thin, crisp almond wafers.

250 g/5 large eggs

1¼ t plus pinch of fine sea salt

163 g/¾ cup honey

163 g/¾ cup plus 1 T granulated sugar

234 g/1⅔ cups whole-grain spelt flour

234 g/1⅔ cups whole-grain Kamut flour

425 g/3 cups skin-on raw almonds

57 g/½ cup whole dried hibiscus flowers, roughly chopped (available at health food stores or Mexican markets)

Zest of 3 or 4 bergamots or a mix of lemon and orange zest (optional)

Preheat the oven to 350°F/180°C. In the bowl of a stand mixer fitted with the whisk attachment, whip 200 g/4 of the eggs and 1¼ teaspoons of the salt on medium speed. Slowly add the honey and sugar. When all of the sugar has been incorporated, turn the speed to high and beat for 5 to 8 minutes, until the mixture falls from the beater in ribbons.

Turn the mixer off and switch to the paddle attachment. With the mixer on low speed, add both flours in two additions, followed by the almonds, hibiscus flowers, and bergamot zest; mix until just combined.

Moisten your hands with a little water to keep the dough from sticking to them. On a parchment-lined baking sheet, form the dough into two logs, each approximately 3 in/7.5 cm wide, 16 in/40 cm long, and 1 in/2.5 cm tall, spacing the logs 3 in/7.5 cm apart.

In a small bowl, whisk the remaining 50 g/1 egg with the remaining pinch of salt then brush the egg wash over the surface of both logs.

Bake for 20 minutes, rotate the baking sheet, then bake an additional 10 minutes, until the logs are golden brown. Transfer the logs to a cooling rack and let cool. With a serrated knife, cut into ⅛-in/4-mm slices, then lay the slices on two parchment-lined baking sheets.

Bake the sliced cookies for 6 to 10 minutes, until golden brown and crisp, rotating the baking sheets halfway through baking. Let cool. The cookies will keep for 1 to 2 weeks in an airtight container.

Yield: Six dozen cookies

SALTED CHOCOLATE– RYE COOKIES

Rye has proven a fine substitute for wheat in cookie applications, adding a distinguishing flavor that is naturally complementary to chocolate and a tender texture. Rye doughs can be especially delicate to work with; this fudgy cookie seasoned with salt is an easy place to start.

454 g/2⅔ cups chopped bittersweet chocolate (70%), preferably Valrhona

57 g/4 T unsalted butter

85 g/¾ cup whole-grain dark rye flour

1 t baking powder

½ t salt

200 g/4 large eggs, at room temperature

340 g/1½ cups muscovado sugar

1 T vanilla extract

Good-quality sea salt, such as Maldon or flaky fleur de sel, for topping

Place a saucepan filled with 1 in/2.5 cm of water over medium heat and bring to a simmer. Set a heatproof bowl over simmering water, taking care that the bottom of the bowl is not touching the water, and melt together the chocolate and butter, stirring occasionally. Once melted, remove from the heat and let cool slightly.

In a small bowl, whisk together the flour, baking powder, and salt and set aside.

Place the eggs in the bowl of a stand mixer fitted with the whisk attachment. Whip on medium-high speed, adding the sugar a little bit at a time, until all the sugar is incorporated. Turn the mixer to high and whip until the eggs have nearly tripled in volume, about 6 minutes.

Reduce the mixer speed to low and add the melted chocolate-butter mixture and the vanilla. Mix to combine, scraping down the sides of the bowl as needed, then mix in the flour mixture just until combined. At this point the dough will be very soft and loose, which is normal; it will firm up as it chills.

Refrigerate the dough in the mixing bowl until it is just firm to the touch, about 30 minutes (the longer you chill the dough, the harder it is to scoop; if it chills for more than an hour, remove the dough from the fridge to warm up to room temperature before scooping).

Preheat the oven to 350°F/180°C and line two baking sheets with parchment paper. Remove the dough from the fridge and scoop with a rounded tablespoon onto the baking sheets, spacing the balls of dough 2 in/5 cm apart. Top each mound of dough with a few flakes of sea salt, pressing gently so it adheres. Bake for 8 to 10 minutes, until the cookies have completely puffed up and

have a smooth bottom and rounded top. Remove the baking sheets from the oven and let cool slightly (the cookies may flatten a bit when cooling), then transfer to a wire rack and let cool completely. The cookies will keep up to 3 days in an airtight container.

Yield: Four dozen small cookies

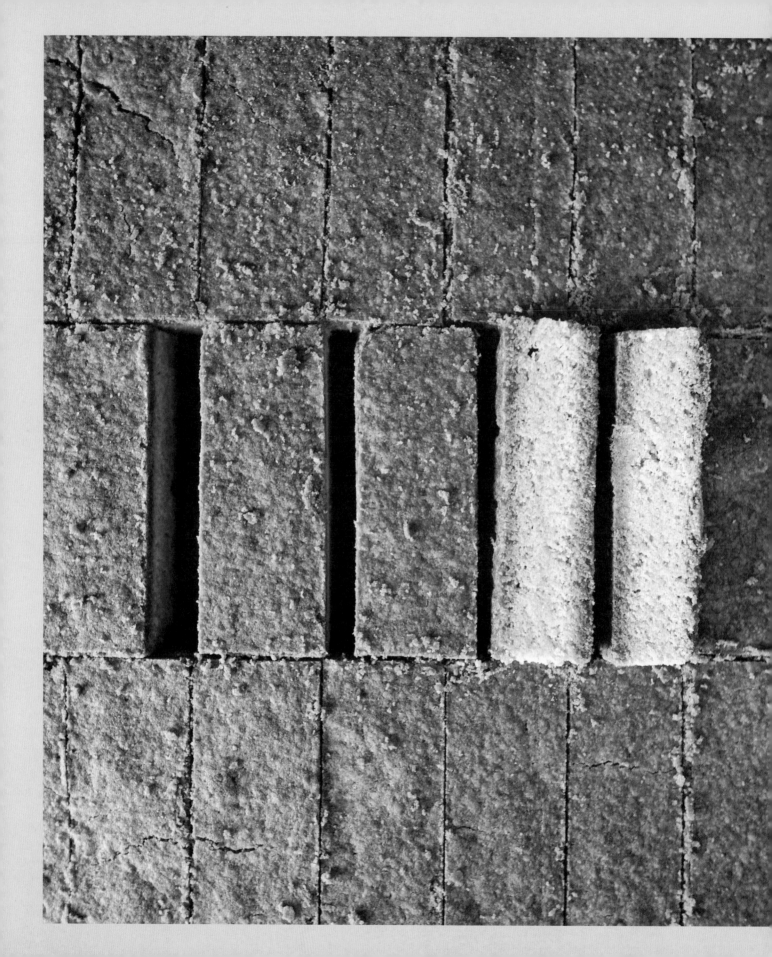

CHAMOMILE-KAMUT SHORTBREAD

This delicate, golden shortbread is made with whole-grain Kamut flour. Chamomile flowers, along with honey and lemon, are infused into the butter.

53 g/¼ cup honey

10 g/4 T dried chamomile flowers

255 g/1 cup plus 2 T unsalted butter, very soft

255 g/1¾ cups whole-grain Kamut flour

75 g/½ cup plus 2 T cornstarch

½ t fine sea salt or kosher salt

110 g/½ cup sugar

Zest of 3 lemons

Preheat the oven to 350°F/180°C. Line a rimmed baking sheet or 6-by-10-in/15-by-25-cm glass baking dish with parchment paper.

In a small saucepan over medium heat, warm the honey. Add the chamomile flowers in a tea strainer or satchel, remove from the heat, and let steep for 30 minutes, until cool. Remove the chamomile and discard.

Put the butter in the bowl of a stand mixer fitted with the paddle attachment (the butter must be very soft, the consistency of mayonnaise or whipped cream). Mix on medium speed until well combined.

Sift the flour, cornstarch, and salt together into a bowl. Add 55 g/¼ cup of the sugar to the butter and mix on high speed for 5 to 8 minutes until very light, fluffy, pale and doubled in volume. Add the flour mixture and mix just until a smooth dough forms, then fold in the lemon zest and chamomile flowers.

Pat the dough evenly into the prepared pan. Bake for 15 to 20 minutes, until the top and bottom are golden brown. Let cool on a wire rack until warm to the touch.

Finish the shortbread by dusting the surface with the remaining sugar. Tilt the dish so that the sugar fully and evenly coats the surface, then carefully tip out any excess sugar.

While the cookies are still warm, with a thin, sharp knife, cut the shortbread into rectangular fingers about ½ in/2.5 cm wide and 2 in/5 cm long. (If the cookies have become cold they will not slice well, so they must still be warm when you cut them.) Refrigerate the cookies for at least 1 hour before removing them from the baking dish.

The first cookie is difficult to remove, but the rest should come out easily with the aid of a small offset spatula. The cookies will keep for up to 2 weeks in an airtight container.

Yield: Five dozen small cookies

PECAN SHORTBREAD

A sort of pecan sandie, this shortbread is made with whole-grain Kamut flour, which produces the most sandy-textured shortbread of any of the alternative flours. Pecans have been a favorite of mine since I was a kid growing up in Texas. Unrefined maple sugar in combination with these rich nuts results in a whole-food classic.

212 g/2 cups pecans

212 g/1½ cups Kamut flour

½ t baking powder

¼ t fine sea salt

114 g/½ cup unsalted butter, at room temperature

113 g/½ cup plus 3 T maple sugar

1 t vanilla extract

60 g/3 T maple syrup for brushing (optional)

Preheat the oven to 350°F/180°C. Spread the pecans in a single layer on a baking sheet and toast until golden brown, about 7 minutes. Remove from the oven and allow to cool completely.

In the bowl of a food processor, pulse the pecans and flour together until the pecans are finely ground, about 1 minute. Transfer to a bowl and whisk in the baking powder and salt.

In the bowl of a stand mixer fitted with the paddle attachment, beat the butter and maple sugar on medium-high speed until light and creamy, about 3 minutes. Reduce the mixer speed to low, add the vanilla and the flour-pecan mixture, and mix until the dough comes together into a cohesive mass.

Roll the dough into walnut-size balls and transfer to two parchment-lined baking sheets, spacing the balls about 1½ in/4 cm apart.

Bake for 18 to 20 minutes, rotating the baking sheets halfway through baking, until the edges of the cookies are golden. Remove the baking sheets from the oven and, using a pastry brush, brush the cookies with maple syrup (if desired). Let cool completely on the baking sheets. The cookies will keep for up to 1 week in an airtight container.

Yield: Three dozen cookies

BARLEY-WALNUT-FIG COOKIES

Whole-grain barley dough is high in protein and, in combination with walnuts, makes an exceptionally tender, nutrient-dense crust. The fig filling is judiciously spiced with cinnamon and flavored with lemon zest and brandy. This crust and filling can be used to make a filled log-style cookie, as directed here, which is sliced and baked, or to make filled thumbprint cookies.

BARLEY WALNUT DOUGH

68 g/½ cup walnuts

181 g/¾ cup plus 1 T unsalted butter, at room temperature

68 g/⅓ cup plus 1 T sucanat

50 g/1 large egg, at room temperature

272 g/2⅓ cups whole-grain barley flour

Pinch of fine sea salt

FIG FILLING

454 g/3 cups dried mission figs, stems removed and discarded, roughly chopped

300 ml/1⅓ cups water

40 g/2 T plus 2 t sugar

1 cinnamon stick

255 g/2⅔ cups walnuts, toasted and finely chopped

Zest of 1 lemon

1 t brandy (optional)

EGG WASH

50 g/1 large egg

Pinch of fine sea salt

55 g/¼ cup sugar

Preheat the oven to 350°F/180°C. Spread the walnuts in a single layer on a baking sheet and toast until golden brown, about 7 minutes. Remove from oven and allow to cool, then finely chop.

To make the dough: In the bowl of a stand mixer fitted with the paddle attachment, beat the butter and sucanat on medium speed until smooth. Add the egg and beat until smooth.

Stop the mixer and scrape down the sides of the bowl with a rubber spatula. Add the flour, ground walnuts, and salt all at once and mix on low speed until just incorporated.

On a lightly floured work surface, evenly divide the dough and form into two rectangles, each about ½ in/12 mm thick. Wrap in plastic and refrigerate for at least 2 hours or up to overnight.

To make the filling: In a medium nonreactive saucepan, add the figs, water, sugar, and cinnamon stick. Bring to a simmer over medium-high heat and poach the figs until tender and hydrated, about 15 minutes. Remove from the heat and cool to room temperature; remove and discard the cinnamon stick. Transfer the figs with their soaking water to a food processor; add the walnuts, lemon zest, and brandy (if using); and process until smooth. Lay out two large rectangles of plastic wrap, each 20 in/50 cm long, on your work surface and divide the fig mixture evenly between them. Form into 2-by-16-in/5-by-40-cm rectangles, wrap tightly, and refrigerate for 30 minutes.

Remove one portion of dough from the refrigerator and transfer to a lightly floured work surface. With a lightly floured rolling pin, roll the dough into a 6-by-16-in/15-by-40-cm rectangle. Place one rectangle of the fig mixture directly onto the dough, centering it. Fold one side of the dough up and over the fig filling, then repeat with the other side, overlapping the dough slightly and pressing gently to seal. Place seam-side down on a parchment-lined baking sheet. Repeat with the remaining dough and fig filling, placing the finished log alongside the first on the same baking sheet.

To make the egg wash: In a small bowl, whisk together the egg and salt.

Brush the exterior of both logs with the egg wash and top with the sugar. Bake in the center of the oven for 25 to 30 minutes, rotating the baking sheet halfway through baking, until golden brown. Remove from the oven, let cool on the baking sheet for 15 minutes, then slice with a serrated knife into 1-in/2.5-cm slices. The cookies will keep for 3 to 5 days in an airtight container.

Yield: Three dozen cookies

PILONCILLO-NIB ROCHERS

Piloncillo, or *panela*, is unrefined cane sugar that is often found in cone form. Used in both sweet and savory preparations, this evaporated cane juice is found in Mexico and Central and South America. The classic Tartine rocher recipe gains a much more complex caramel flavor profile when using the *piloncillo* in place of refined white sugar; whole cocoa nibs add flavor and texture. If your *piloncillo* is very moist, spread it on a baking sheet and place it the oven overnight to dry out slightly. The pilot light and cool, dry environment will do the job.

120 g/4 egg whites, at room temperature
230 g/2 cups piloncillo sugar
Pinch of fine sea salt
120 g/½ cup cocoa nibs
½ t vanilla extract

Preheat the oven to 350°F/180°C. Line two baking sheets with parchment paper.

Place a saucepan of water over medium heat and bring to a simmer. In a large heatproof bowl, whisk together the egg whites, piloncillo, and salt. Set the bowl over the simmering water, taking care that the bottom of the bowl is not touching the water. Continue to whisk until the whites are hot to the touch (registering 120°F/48°C on an instant-read thermometer), about 5 minutes.

Transfer the egg white mixture to the bowl of a stand mixer fitted with the whisk attachment. Beat on high speed for 5 to 7 minutes until the mixture is very thick and holds glossy, stiff peaks when you lift the beater. With a rubber spatula, fold in the cocoa nibs and vanilla.

With a small ice-cream scoop or two tablespoons, immediately scoop the meringue into mounds that are 1½ in/4 cm in diameter on two parchment-lined baking sheets.

Place the baking sheets in the oven and keep the oven door ajar with the handle of a wooden spoon to allow moisture to escape. Bake the cookies for 15 to 20 minutes, until they puff slightly, crack along the sides, and feel dry on the outside but soft to the touch. They will harden as they cool. Transfer the cookies to a wire rack and let cool. The cookies will keep for up to 2 weeks in an airtight container.

Yield: Three dozen cookies

PEANUT BUTTER COOKIES

Peanut butter and toasted sesame butter both make impossibly rich, densely flavorful cookies. I like to keep these around as small bites, good for eating on their own or for sandwiching with very dark chocolate ganache or tart concentrated berry or apricot jam.

155 g/1 cup peanuts

155 g/1⅓ cups oat flour

½ t baking powder

1 t salt

57 g/¼ cup unsalted butter, at room temperature

100 g/½ cup sugar

128 g/½ cup good-quality smooth natural peanut butter

1 t vanilla extract

Preheat the oven to 350°F/180°C. Spread the peanuts in a single layer on a baking sheet and toast until golden brown, 5 to 7 minutes. Remove from the oven and let cool completely.

In the bowl of a food processor, pulse the peanuts and flour together until very finely ground. Transfer to a bowl and whisk in the baking powder and salt.

In the bowl of a stand mixer fitted with the paddle attachment, beat the butter and sugar on medium-high speed until well combined and beginning to gain volume, about 2 minutes.

Add the peanut butter and beat to combine on medium speed, scraping down the sides of the bowl as needed. Reduce the mixer speed to low and add the vanilla.

With the mixer speed on low, add the flour-nut mixture and mix until just combined.

Roll the dough into walnut-size balls, and transfer them to two parchment-lined baking sheets, spacing them 1 in/2.5 cm apart. Bake for 15 to 18 minutes, rotating the baking sheets midway through baking, until the edges of the cookies are golden.

Remove the baking sheets from the oven and let the cookies cool completely. Repeat with the remaining dough. The cookies will keep for up to 3 days in an airtight container.

Yield: Five dozen small cookies

SESAME VARIATION

Replace the peanuts with 147 g/⅔ cup sesame seeds, the oat flour with 147 g/1 cup whole-grain Kamut flour, the peanut butter with 128 g/½ cup tahini. Reduce the salt by half and proceed as directed.

50/50 SABLÉ COOKIES

The idea of the 50/50 sablé came in the midst of a blizzard of cookie testing, and the recipe is loosely based on a traditional sablé ratio, representing roughly equal amounts of whole-grain flour and nut flour. One afternoon I walked into the bakery to find an array of sablés, all made using different types of whole-grain flour paired with a different nut or seed. I think of these base ratio recipes as building blocks; the finished cookies are good as is, but very simple. We start with the base sablés, and fill or sandwich them with jam, citrus cream, chocolate, or sweetened nut butter. Almost all the combinations of flour and nuts we tried yielded fine sablés, so at a certain point it was necessary to simply choose a few favorites to present here. The flavor combinations that follow are examples that worked well together and suited my taste: cashew with barley flour, pecan with rye flour, pistachio with brown rice flour, pumpkin seed with Kamut flour, and cocoa nib with buckwheat flour. Try using different types of sugars, and add spices or aromatics to suit your own taste. Here, the amounts for the nuts and flours are given in grams only, rather than grams and U.S. measurements, since the U.S. measurements vary depending on the specific nut and flour that you choose.

186 g nuts, pumpkin seeds, or cocoa nibs

186 g flour

133 g/⅔ cup sugar

¼ t fine sea salt

133 g/½ cup plus 1 T unsalted butter, cut into pieces at room temperature

Preheat the oven to 350°F/180°C. Spread the nuts or pumpkin seeds on a baking sheet and toast until golden in color. (Cocoa nibs are already toasted, so if making the cocoa nib–buckwheat version, skip this step.) Remove from the oven and let cool completely.

In the bowl of a food processor, combine the nuts, pumpkin seeds, or cocoa nibs, flour, sugar, and salt and pulse until very finely ground, about 1 minute. Transfer to a large bowl and add the butter by hand, a few pieces at a time, massaging the butter into the dry ingredients until it forms a dough. (If the dough seems dry and is not holding together, add water, 1 tablespoon at a time, until the dough comes together.)

Turn the dough out onto a lightly floured work surface and bring it together with your hands into one cohesive mass.

Roll the dough into two logs, each about 15 by ½ in/38 cm by 12 mm, then cut each log into ½-in/12-mm slices and roll each slice into a ball. Transfer the balls, spacing them about ½ in/12 mm apart, to parchment-lined baking sheets.

Bake for 10 to 12 minutes, rotating the baking sheets halfway through baking to ensure even browning, until the cookies are golden around the edges (depending on the nut-flour combination used, the golden hue will be more or less noticeable; with the cocoa nib and buckwheat combination it will be less noticeable, with the cashew-barley combination, more).

Remove the baking sheets from the oven and let the cookies cool completely. The cookies will keep up to 3 days in an airtight container.

Yield: About five dozen cookies

FAVORITE SABLÉ VARIATIONS

Pumpkin Seed–Kamut: Replace nuts with 186 g/1⅓ cups pumpkin seeds and use 186 g/1⅓ cups whole-grain Kamut flour.

Cocoa Nib–Buckwheat: Replace nuts with 186 g/1½ cups cocoa nibs and use 186 g/1⅓ cups whole-grain buckwheat flour.

Cashew-Barley: Replace nuts with 186 g/1⅔ cups cashews and use 186 g/1⅔ cups whole-grain barley flour.

Pecan-Rye: Replace nuts with 186 g/1⅔ cups pecans and use 186 g/1½ cups whole-grain dark rye flour.

Pistachio–Brown Rice: Replace nuts with 186 g/1½ cups pistachios and use 186 g/1 cup brown rice flour.

BUCKWHEAT-HAZELNUT SABLÉS

In these delicate cookies, the earthy flavor of whole-grain buckwheat is rounded out by the rich toasted hazelnuts. Citrus zest adds the high notes. It's important to process the nuts only until coarsely ground, which gives the finished cookies the tender, lacy texture that distinguishes them from denser, sandier 50/50 Sablé Cookies (page 258).

150 g/1 cup raw, skinned hazelnuts

100 g /¾ cup buckwheat flour

½ t fine sea salt

200 g/¾ cup plus 2 T unsalted butter, at room temperature

100 g/½ cup coconut sugar

40 g/2 large egg yolks

Zest of 1 lemon

Zest of 1 orange

Preheat the oven to 350°F/180°C. Spread the hazelnuts on a baking sheet and toast until golden brown, 5 to 7 minutes. Remove from the oven and let cool completely.

Put the cooled hazelnuts and half of the flour in a food processor and pulse until uniformly chopped and the mixture looks pebbly.

Take care not to overprocess; the nuts should not be finely ground. Transfer to a medium bowl, add the remaining flour and the salt, and stir to combine.

In the bowl of a stand mixer fitted with the paddle attachment, beat the butter and coconut sugar on medium-high speed until just combined but not gained much volume, 1 to 2 minutes.

Reduce the mixer speed to low and slowly add the egg yolks, one at a time, scraping down the bowl after each addition. Add the lemon and orange zests and mix to combine. Add half of the nut-flour mixture and mix until just combined. Scrape down the bowl, then add the remaining flour mixture and continue mixing until the dough comes together into a ball.

Form the dough into a 14-in/35-cm log about 2½ in/6 cm in diameter, wrap tightly in plastic, and refrigerate for 1 hour. Line two baking sheets with parchment paper. Slice the log into ¼-in/6-mm coins and transfer to the prepared baking sheets, spacing them about 1½ in/4 cm apart. Bake for about 15 minutes, rotating the pans halfway through baking until the cookies are golden brown and fragrant. Remove the baking sheets from the oven and let the cookies cool for 1 minute, then transfer to a wire rack and let cool completely. The sablés will keep for up to 5 days in an airtight container.

Yield: About two dozen cookies

CHEDDAR CHEESE SABLÉS

Both savory sablé recipes reference the cheese crackers from our first book, *Tartine*. Liz's crackers are reworked slightly here to make two additional variations: each uses a different whole-grain flour, nut, and cheese to yield tender sablés with distinct flavors.

100 g/¾ cup plus 2 T whole-grain barley flour

70 g/½ cup pine nuts

1 t fine sea salt

1 t chopped fresh savory or marjoram

1 t fresh thyme leaves

¾ t freshly ground black pepper

225 g/2 cups sharp Cheddar cheese, coarsely grated

55 g/¼ cup unsalted butter, at room temperature

20 g/1 T plus 1 t leaven (see page 35)

30 g/2 T whole cumin

30 g/2 T caraway seeds

30 g/2 T white sesame seeds

30 g/2 T poppy seeds

In a medium bowl, combine the flour, pine nuts, salt, savory, thyme, and black pepper. In a large bowl, add the Cheddar, butter, and leaven and mix to combine. Add the flour mixture to the cheese-butter mixture and stir until well combined. Refrigerate for 15 minutes.

Transfer the dough to a lightly floured work surface and roll into a log about 2½ by 8 in/ 5 by 20 cm. In a small bowl, combine the cumin, caraway seeds, sesame seeds, and poppy seeds. Spread the seed mixture onto your work surface and roll the log of dough in it, pressing lightly so the seeds adhere, until completely covered on all sides. Wrap the dough tightly with plastic and refrigerate for 1 hour. Line two baking sheets with parchment paper.

Preheat the oven to 350°F/180°C. Cut the log of dough into ⅛-in/4-mm slices. Transfer the slices to the prepared baking sheets and bake for 8 to 10 minutes, rotating the baking sheets halfway through baking, until the edges of the crackers are golden brown. Transfer the crackers to a wire cooling rack. The sablés will keep for 1 week in an airtight container.

Yield: About three dozen sablés

BLUE CHEESE SABLÉS

Depending on the cheese you are using, you may need to adjust the salt slightly in the recipe. Sablés could not be simpler: the dough comes together in less than 10 minutes.

100 g/¾ cup plus 2 T oat flour

70 g/⅓ cup walnuts, chopped medium-fine

¾ t fine sea salt

1 t chopped fresh sage

¾ t freshly ground black pepper

225 g/2 cups crumbled medium-soft blue cheese

55 g/¼ cup unsalted butter, at room temperature

20 g/1 T plus 1 t leaven (see page 35)

30 g/2 T whole cumin

30 g/2 T caraway seeds

30 g/2 T white sesame seeds

30 g/2 T poppy seeds

30 g/2 T anise seeds

In a medium bowl, combine the flour, walnuts, salt, sage, and black pepper. In a large bowl, add the cheese, butter, and leaven and mix to combine. Add the flour mixture to the cheese-butter mixture and stir until well combined. Refrigerate for 15 minutes.

Transfer the dough to a lightly floured work surface and roll into a log about 2½ by 8 in/ 6 by 20 cm. In a small bowl, combine the cumin, caraway seeds, sesame seeds, poppy seeds, and anise seeds. Spread the seed mixture onto your work surface and roll the log of dough in it, pressing lightly so the seeds adhere, until completely covered on all sides. Wrap the dough tightly with plastic and refrigerate for 1 hour. Line two baking sheets with parchment paper.

Preheat the oven to 350°F/180°C. Cut the log of dough into ⅛-in/4-mm slices. Transfer the slices to the prepared baking sheets and bake for 8 to 10 minutes, rotating the baking sheets halfway through baking, until the edges of the crackers are golden brown. Transfer the crackers to a wire cooling rack. The sablés will keep for 1 week in an airtight container.

Yield: About three dozen sablés

SWEET PÂTE À CHOUX DOUGH

Relying more on eggs and less on flour to add structure to the dough, pâte à choux is well suited to whole-grain flours. Swapping Kamut or spelt flour produced very similar results to our standard Tartine recipe but with an added layer of flavor from the less-refined flour. Barley worked as well but was slightly denser.

228 ml/1 cup nonfat milk

¼ t fine sea salt

1 t sugar

115 g/½ cup unsalted butter

140 g/1 cup whole-grain spelt or Kamut flour

250 g/5 large eggs, at room temperature

In a medium, heavy-bottomed saucepan, combine the milk, salt, sugar, and butter and place over medium heat until the butter melts and the mixture comes to just under a boil. Add the flour all at once, stirring vigorously with a wooden spoon. Keep stirring until the mixture has formed a smooth mass, pulls away from the sides of the pan, and some of the moisture has evaporated, about 3 minutes.

Transfer the dough to the bowl of a stand mixer fitted with the paddle attachment or to a heatproof mixing bowl. If using a mixer, add the eggs, one at a time, and mix on medium-high speed, incorporating each egg before adding the next. When all the eggs have been added, the mixture will be thick, smooth, and shiny. If mixing by hand, add the eggs, one at a time, and mix with a wooden spoon, incorporating each egg before adding the next. Use immediately (once piped or baked, the dough can be frozen).

Yield: 680 g/2½ cups dough

ÉCLAIRS

Rather than filling these pastries with classic pastry cream, we experimented with making nut milks, then developed a recipe for pastry cream made with the nut milks. The hazelnut milk pastry cream used here is complemented by a bittersweet chocolate ganache.

1 recipe Sweet Pâte à Choux Dough (facing page)
1 recipe Nut Milk Pastry Cream (page 327), made with Hazelnut Nut Milk

GANACHE

115 g/⅔ cup chopped bittersweet chocolate (70%), preferably Valrhona
115 g/½ cup heavy cream

Preheat the oven to 425°F/220°C. Fill a pastry bag fitted with a ½-in/12-mm (number 6 or 7) plain tip with pâte a choux dough. Line two baking sheets with parchment paper. Pipe out fingers of dough, each about 5 in/12 cm long and 1 in/2.5 cm wide, spacing them about 2 in/5 cm apart. If you end up with a bulge or a "tail" at the end of the piping, smooth it over with a damp fingertip.

Bake for 10 minutes, until puffed and light golden brown. Reduce the oven temperature to 375°F/190°C and continue to bake until the shells feel light for their size and are hollow inside, about 12 minutes longer. They should be nicely browned all over. Remove from the oven and let cool on wire racks. They should be used as soon as they are cool enough to fill. (You can also store them in an airtight container and freeze them for up to 1 month. When you are ready to fill them, recrisp them directly from the freezer in a 450°F/230°C oven for about 10 minutes, then let cool before filling.)

To make the ganache: Place a saucepan of water over medium heat and bring to a simmer. Set a heatproof bowl over the water, taking care that the bottom of the bowl does not touch the water. Add the chocolate and heat until halfway melted. Stir gently, remove from heat and let cool until it registers between 95°F/35°C and 115°F/45°C on an instant-read thermometer.

In a separate medium saucepan over medium-high heat, bring the cream to just under a boil; do not let the temperature of the cream exceed 140°F/60°C. Add the hot cream to the chocolate in four or five additions, using a heatproof spatula to incorporate the cream and chocolate using vigorous strokes. The temperature of mixture should not exceed 113°F/43°C, which is why the cream is added in several additions. The mixture may appear broken at first but should come together by the final addition of cream to be smooth and glossy. Let cool slightly. With a hand-held immersion blender, blend the ganache until completely smooth and uniform. Use immediately.

Stir the pastry cream until smooth and then spoon the cream into a pastry bag fitted with a ½-in/12-mm (number 6 or 7) plain tip. It is easiest to start with a hole in each end of the shell and to fill from both ends if necessary. (Sometimes pockets inside the shell prevent the pastry cream from filling the entire shell from a single hole.) Fill the shells until they feel heavy. Dip the top of each filled éclair into the ganache, shaking gently to allow the excess to drip off, then place upright on a wire rack and allow the ganache to set.

Alternatively, you can fill the shells by splitting them in half with a serrated knife. Dip the top half in the ganache, allowing the excess to drip off, and then place upright on a wire rack and allow the ganache to set. Spoon the pastry cream into the bottoms of the shells and cap with the glazed tops. Serve the pastries at once or refrigerate for up to 6 hours. They should be eaten the same day they are filled.

Yield: Twelve éclairs

PETS DE NONNES

The most well-known (and loved) fried doughnut made of pâte à choux is the French cruller. Pets de Nonnes, or "nuns toots," are basically doughnut holes made with choux paste. They can be tossed in any flavored sugar; my Scandinavian travels left me with a strong taste for fresh cracked cardamom—an assertive spice—to flavor the rich, eggy fried dough.

1 recipe Sweet Pâte à Choux Dough (page 264)

Grapeseed oil for frying

200 g/1 cup sugar

1 T ground cardamom

Fill a pastry bag fitted with a ½-in/12-mm (number 6 or 7) tip with pâte à choux dough. Line two baking sheets with parchment paper. Pipe the dough into mounds about 1 in/2.5 cm in diameter, spacing them as close together as possible without touching. Freeze for 2 to 3 hours, until solid.

In a wide, heavy-bottomed pot, heat a 2-in/ 5-cm depth of oil over medium-high heat, until it registers 375°F/190°C on a deep-frying thermometer. While the oil heats, in a medium bowl, combine the sugar and cardamom. Set aside.

Preheat the oven to 200°F/95°C. Remove one baking sheet of dough from the freezer and gently transfer six or seven frozen dough balls into the hot oil using a slotted spoon. As they fry, they'll transform into somewhat irregular shapes; they are done when they are deep golden brown and float, 8 to 10 minutes. Remove from the oil with the slotted spoon and transfer to a paper towel–lined plate to drain, then transfer to the bowl containing the sugar mixture and toss to coat. Transfer to a wire rack set over a baking sheet and place in the oven to keep warm while you fry the remaining dough balls.

Let the oil return to 375°F/190°C, then repeat with the remaining dough and spiced sugar. Serve warm.

Yield: About four dozen pets de nonnes

SAVORY PÂTE À CHOUX DOUGH

Rye, which we use for a variation of this savory dough, is a less intuitive choice, and yields the most interesting choux dough. Dark rye flour used in combination with unsweetened cocoa powder makes a chocolate brown–colored dough. The same rye-cocoa mixure produced similarly colored savory gougères. This selection of sweet and savory applications illustrates the range.

310 ml/1¼ cups nonfat milk

140 g/¼ cup plus 2 T unsalted butter

1 t fine sea salt

140 g/1 cup whole-grain spelt or Kamut flour

250 g/5 large eggs, at room temperature

In a medium heavy-bottomed saucepan, combine the milk, butter, and salt and place over medium heat until the butter melts and the mixture comes to just under a boil. Add the flour all at once, stirring vigorously with a wooden spoon. Keep stirring until the mixture has formed a smooth mass, pulls away from the sides of the pan, and some of the moisture has evaporated, about 3 minutes.

Transfer the dough to the bowl of a stand mixer fitted with the paddle attachment or to a heatproof mixing bowl. If using a mixer, add the eggs, one at a time, and mix on medium-high speed, incorporating each egg before adding the next. When all the eggs have been added, the mixture will be very thick, smooth, and shiny. If mixing by hand, add the eggs, one at a time, to the bowl and mix with a wooden spoon, incorporating each egg before adding the next. Use immediately (once piped or baked, the dough can be frozen).

Yield: 680 g/2¾ cups dough

RYE-COCOA VARIATION

Substitute 140 g/1 cup plus 22 g/3 T whole-grain dark rye flour for the spelt or Kamut flour, and add 15 g/3 T unsweetened cocoa powder along with the flour.

GOUGÈRES

Made with dark rye flour and unsweet-ened cocoa and loaded with cheese and fresh herbs, these oversized puffs are whole-grain versions of the ones we've made in the bakery since the beginning. Split and fill with cured meats and bitter greens to make a quick, satisfying lunch enjoyed with a cool dry rosé or hoppy ale.

115 g/¾ cup grated Comté or Gruyère cheese

1 t freshly ground black pepper

1½ t minced fresh marjoram

1 recipe Rye-Cocoa Pâte à Choux Dough (see variation, facing page)

1½ t minced fresh thyme leaves

EGG WASH

50 g/1 large egg

Pinch of fine sea salt

Preheat the oven to 425°F/220°C. Line a baking sheet with parchment paper. Add 75 g/½ cup of the cheese, the pepper, the marjoram, and the thyme to the pâte à choux dough and stir well with a rubber spatula to incorporate.

Transfer the dough to a pastry bag fitted with a ½-in/12-mm (number 6 or 7) tip. Pipe 1-in/2.5-cm mounds onto the prepared baking sheet, spacing them about 1½ in/4 cm apart, or use a spoon to drop the dough in 1-in/2.5-cm mounds.

To make the egg wash: In a small bowl, whisk together the egg and salt.

Lightly brush the top of each dough mound with the egg wash, then top with the remaining 40 g/¼ cup cheese, dividing evenly.

Bake for 25 to 30 minutes, until puffed, golden brown, and light for their size, rotating the baking sheet after 20 minutes to ensure even browning. These are delicious served hot or warm and they are also good at room temperature. Or let cool completely, store in the refrigerator for up to a few days in an airtight container, and recrisp in a 350°F/180°C oven for 5 minutes before serving.

Note: You can also form the gougères on the baking sheet, place in the freezer until frozen, and then transfer them to an airtight container and freeze for up to 1 month. Bake them straight from the freezer on a buttered or parchment-lined baking sheet. Brush the tops lightly with the egg wash, sprinkle with cheese before baking, and increase the baking time by about 10 minutes.

Yield: Four dozen gougères

LARGE-SIZED GOUGÈRES VARIATION

To make 4-in/10-cm gougères, use a large spoon to form 3-in/7.5-cm rounds about 1 in/2.5 cm high on the prepared baking sheet, spacing them about 2 in/5 cm apart. Brush with the egg wash and top with the cheese. Bake for 35 to 45 minutes, until they are golden brown and puffed, light for their size. Remove from the oven and poke a small hole in the side of each pastry to allow steam to escape. Releasing the steam keeps them from collapsing (this step is unnecessary for the small ones). If splitting and filling, let cool to room temperature; otherwise, they may be served hot, warm, or at room temperature.

Yield: Eight to ten gougères

POMMES DAUPHINES

These fried potato puffs land somewhere between the French fry and the hush puppy: crisp and golden on the exterior, custardy inside, expressing the contrast I'm after in so many foods, from bread to éclairs. Delicious with a crush of sea salt, even better with spicy mustard aïoli.

1.13 kg/about 4 large russet potatoes

1 recipe Savory Pâte à Choux Dough
(page 268)

1 T freshly ground black pepper

1 T salt

20 g/2 T minced fresh thyme leaves

Grapeseed oil for frying

Grainy mustard for serving

Preheat the oven to 400°F/200°C. Rinse the potatoes and pierce all over with a fork, then transfer to the oven and bake for 45 minutes to 1 hour, until a knife easily penetrates the potatoes. Remove from the oven, carefully cut each potato in half, and let cool completely. Once cool, scoop the flesh out of each potato and discard the skins or save for another use.

In a large bowl, add the pâte à choux dough, black pepper, salt, and thyme and stir with a rubber spatula until well combined. Add the cooled potatoes and mix until a cohesive dough forms. (The dough can be prepared a day ahead. Cover tightly with plastic and refrigerate overnight; allow it to come to room temperature before it's fried.)

In a large, heavy-bottomed pot over medium-high heat, heat a 2-in/5-cm depth of oil until it registers 375°F/190°C on a deep-frying thermometer. Preheat the oven to 200°F/95°C.

Using two tablespoons, carefully drop rounded mounds of dough into the hot oil, taking care not to crowd the pot (they expand slightly when fried). Fry the balls for 5 to 7 minutes, turning them with tongs so they brown on all sides, until golden brown. Remove from the oil with a slotted spoon and transfer to a paper towel–lined plate to drain, then transfer to a baking sheet and place in the oven to keep warm. Let the oil return to 375°F/190°C, then repeat with the remaining dough.

Just before serving, top the finished puffs with additional salt; serve warm with grainy mustard.

Yield: About four dozen pommes dauphines

271   PASTRY

ZUCCHINI-KUMQUAT TEA CAKE

Whether using butter, as for this or the Banana Tea Cake (see page 276), or olive oil, as for the Apple-Walnut Tea Cake (see page 274), our technique is to cut the fat into the flour, then gently mix in the wet ingredients. Cutting the fat into the flour creates small pockets of air in the finished tea cake as it bakes, yielding a lighter, more tender crumb. This technique is especially well suited to whole-grain or high-extraction flours, which tend to give more dense results. The goal is to offset dense texture with careful technique. Both recipes also incorporate cultured dairy in the form of kefir cream or butter-milk as well as natural leaven to add additional flavor.

88 g/¾ cup walnuts

167 g/1 cup grated zucchini

1¾ t fine sea salt

81g/⅓ cup plus 1 T buttermilk

62 g/¼ cup leaven (page 35)

37 g/2 T plus 1½ t Same-Day Poolish (page 58)

100 g/2 large eggs

59 g/3 T molasses

98 g/½ cup granulated sugar

74 g/½ cup whole-wheat pastry flour

74 g/½ cup high-extraction spelt flour

10 g/1 T plus 1 t baking powder

¾ t baking soda

¾ t ground cinnamon

87 g/6 T cold unsalted butter, cut into cubes

99 g/½ cup Candied Kumquats (recipe follows), strained

Turbinado or Demerera sugar for topping

Preheat the oven to 350°F/180°C. Grease a 9-by-5-in/23-by-12-cm loaf pan (or two 9-by-3-in/13-by-8-cm loaf pans) and line the bottom(s) with parchment paper. Spread the walnuts on a baking sheet and toast until golden brown and fragrant, about 10 minutes. Remove from the oven and let cool, then coarsely chop.

Put the zucchini in a large bowl and toss with 1 teaspoon salt. Let stand for 15 minutes, then pour off any liquid that has accumulated in the bowl. Transfer the grated zucchini to a clean, dry kitchen towel, and squeeze firmly to remove any excess moisture from the zucchini.

In a large bowl, combine the buttermilk, leaven, poolish, eggs, and molasses. In a medium bowl combine the granulated sugar, both flours, baking powder, baking soda, cinnamon, and remaining salt. Add the butter and, using a pastry cutter or bench knife, cut the butter into the flour until the butter pieces are pea-size. Add this mixture to the wet ingredients and mix until just combined. Fold in the walnuts, zucchini, and ¼ cup plus 2 tablespoons of the candied kumquats.

Transfer the batter to the prepared pan(s) and garnish with the remaining kumquats and Turbinado sugar. Bake for 60 to 70 minutes (30 to 40 minutes for miniature loaves), until the cake is dark brown, the kumquats on top are caramelized, and the internal temperature of the cake reads 200°F/95°C. Let cool in the pan(s) for 1 hour, then use a knife to loosen the cake from the pan by slicing around the edges. Unmold onto a wire rack, and let cool completely. The cake will keep at room temperature, wrapped, for up to 3 days.

Yield: One 9-by-5-in/23-by-13-cm loaf cake or two 5-by-3-in/13-by-8-cm miniature loaf cakes

CANDIED KUMQUATS

454 g/4 cups whole kumquats
395 g/2 cups granulated sugar
456 g/2 cups water

Cut the kumquats crosswise into ¼-in/6-mm rounds, discarding the stems and seeds. Cut a piece of parchment paper into a round that is the same diameter as a medium, heavy-bottomed saucepan.

In the saucepan over medium heat, combine the sugar and water and bring to a boil, stirring with a wooden spoon until the sugar dissolves. Add the kumquat slices, cover with the parchment, and weight down with a nonreactive heatproof plate. Reduce the heat until the liquid is gently simmering, then cook until the kumquat slices are tender and translucent, 30 to 45 minutes (the liquid should register about 230°F/100°C on an instant-read thermometer).

Remove from the heat and, using a slotted spoon, transfer the candied kumquats to a heatproof container and ladle syrup over the fruit just to cover; discard any remaining syrup or save for sweetening cocktails. (The syrup will keep, refrigerated, for up to 1 month.) Let the kumquat slices cool completely in the syrup, then refrigerate for up to 1 month.

Yield: 340 g/2 cups candied fruit

APPLE-WALNUT TEA CAKE

375 g/1⅓ cups walnuts

102 g/½ cup leaven (see page 35)

50 g/1 large egg, at room temperature

111 g/½ cup Kefir Cultured Cream or Crème Fraîche (page 245)

129 g/1 cup grated apple

171 g/1¼ cups whole-grain spelt flour

146 g/¾ cup sugar

2¼ t baking powder

¾ t baking soda

¾ t ground cinnamon

½ t fine sea salt

¼ t ground nutmeg

¼ t ground cloves

½ t ground ginger

89 g/¼ cup plus 2 T olive oil

Preheat the oven to 350°F/180°C. Grease a 9-by-5-in/23-by-12-cm loaf pan (or two 5-by-3-in/13-by-8-cm loaf pans) and line the bottom(s) with parchment paper. Spread the walnuts on a baking sheet and toast until golden brown and fragrant, about 10 minutes. Remove from the oven and let cool completely, then coarsely chop.

In a large bowl, mix together the leaven, egg, kefir cream, and grated apple. In a medium bowl, whisk together the flour, sugar, baking powder, baking soda, cinnamon, salt, nutmeg, cloves, and ginger. Add the olive oil to the dry ingredients and, using a bench knife or pastry cutter, cut the oil into the flour until well distributed. Stir in the walnuts, then add the flour and oil mixture to the wet ingredients and stir well to combine.

Transfer the batter to the prepared pan(s). Bake for 60 to 70 minutes (30 to 40 minutes for miniature loaves), or until the internal temperature of the cake reaches 200°F/95°C. Let cool in the pans for 30 minutes, then use a knife to loosen the cake from the pan(s) by slicing around the edges. Unmold onto a wire rack, and let cool completely. The cake will keep at room temperature, wrapped, for up to 3 days.

Yield: One 9-by-5-in/23-by-13-cm loaf cake or two 5-by-3-in/13-by-8-cm miniature loaf cakes

BANANA TEA CAKE

80 g/¾ cup walnuts

170 g/¾ cup mashed ripe but firm banana, plus 1 ripe but firm banana

75 g/⅓ cup buttermilk

56 g/¼ cup leaven (page 35)

53 g/3 T molasses

33 g/3 T Same-Day Poolish (page 58)

100 g/2 large eggs, at room temperature

1 t vanilla extract

68 g/½ cup whole-wheat pastry flour

68 g/½ cup whole-grain spelt flour

80 g/¾ cup granulated sugar

2 t baking powder

1 t baking soda

½ t ground cinnamon

½ t fine sea salt

79 g/⅓ cup cold unsalted butter

133 g/1 cup finely chopped pitted dates

Evaporated cane sugar for topping

Preheat the oven to 350°F/180°C. Grease a 9-by-5-in/23-by-12-cm loaf pan (or two 5-by-3-in/13-by-8-cm loaf pans) and line the bottom(s) with parchment paper. Spread the walnuts on a baking sheet in a single layer and toast until golden brown, about 10 minutes. Remove from the oven, cool completely, then coarsely chop.

In a large bowl, whisk together the mashed banana, buttermilk, leaven, molasses, poolish, eggs, and vanilla. In a medium bowl, combine both flours, the granulated sugar, baking powder, baking soda, cinnamon, and salt. Add the butter and, using a bench knife or pastry cutter, cut the butter into the flour until the butter pieces are pea-size. Mix in the dates and chopped walnuts, rubbing the date pieces into the flour mixture to coat so they don't stick together. Add this mixture to the wet ingredients and stir to combine.

Transfer the batter to the prepared pan(s). Very thinly slice the firm-ripe banana lengthwise and lay the slices lengthwise on top of the tea cake. Finish by topping with the cane sugar.

Bake for 60 to 70 minutes (30 to 40 minutes for miniature loaves), or until the internal temperature of the cake reaches 200°F/95°C. The loaf will be dark brown and the banana slices on top will be caramelized. Let cool in the pan for 30 minutes, then use a knife to loosen the cake from the pan by slicing around the edges. Unmold onto a wire rack, and let cool completely. The cake will keep at room temperature, wrapped, for up to 3 days.

Yield: One 9-by-5-in/23-by-13-cm loaf cake or two 5-by-3-in/13-by-8-cm miniature loaf cakes

LEMON-POPPY-KEFIR POUND CAKE

A classic sort of "quatre-quarts" pound cake, this version is made with whole-grain golden Kamut flour. Cultured kefir butter has a citrusy flavor, a natural pairing with the lemon in the cake; unsalted butter can be substituted.

248 g/1¼ cups granulated sugar

96 g/⅔ cup whole-grain Kamut flour

45 g/⅓ cup white pastry flour

30 g/⅓ cup almond meal

1¼ t baking powder

Pinch of fine sea salt

227 g/1 cup Kefir Butter (page 245) or unsalted butter, cold but pliable

200 g/4 large eggs

30 g/2 T fresh lemon juice

30 g/2 T poppy seeds

Zest of 2 lemons

In the bowl of a stand mixer fitted with the paddle attachment, add the sugar, both flours, almond meal, baking powder, and salt and mix on low speed until just combined. Add the butter, increase the mixer speed to medium, and beat just until fully incorporated. Add the eggs, one at a time, allowing each egg to

be incorporated into the batter before you add the next. Stop the mixer and scrape down the sides of the bowl with a rubber spatula. Turn the mixer to low; slowly add the poppy seeds, lemon juice, and lemon zest; and mix until combined. Cover the bowl tightly with plastic and refrigerate overnight to allow the flours to hydrate.

Preheat the oven to 350°F/180°C. Remove the batter from the refrigerator and let come to room temperature. Grease a 9-by-5-in/ 23-by-12-cm loaf pan (or two 5-by-3-in/ 13-by-8-cm loaf pans) and line the bottom(s) with parchment paper. Spoon the batter into the prepared pan(s), smoothing the top, and bake for 60 to 70 minutes (30 to 40 minutes for miniature loaves), until the top springs back when touched and a toothpick inserted in the center comes out clean.

Let cool in the pan for 30 minutes, then use a knife to loosen the cake from the pan(s) by slicing around the edges. Unmold onto a wire rack, and let cool completely. The cake will keep, at room temperature, wrapped, for 3 days.

Yield: One 9-by-5-in/23-by-13-cm loaf cake or two 5-by-3-in/13-by-8-cm miniature loaf cakes

FRUIT SCONES

To make our sweet and savory scones, we appropriate a technique typically employed to make blitz puff pastry or pie dough to ensure maximum flakiness: a tricky endeavor when using whole-grain flours. The ingredients are thoroughly chilled, butter is rolled into the flour, and the dough is barely mixed together, then loosely laminated to achieve a very flaky pastry. In addition to this technique, the other key here was to find an ideal blend of whole-grain flours that would give the scones the right texture. Oat flour has a natural sweetness and is notably higher in protein and fat than wheat flour but contains no gluten, yielding a rich and exceptionally tender crumb. We use it in combination with whole-wheat pastry flour to give the scones some structure. These recipes include cultured dairy and natural leaven for flavor.

306 g/1 cup plus 5 T cold unsalted butter

312 g/1 ⅓ cups Kefir Cultured Cream or Crème Fraîche (page 245)

306 g/1⅓ cups leaven (page 35)

306 g/1 pint strawberries, raspberries, or blueberries

341 g/2⅓ cups pastry flour

204 g/1¾ cups oat flour

136 g/1 cup plus 1 T whole-wheat pastry flour

1¼ t baking soda

1 T baking powder

102 g/½ cup granulated sugar

2 t plus pinch of fine sea salt

Zest of 10 lemons

50 g/1 large egg

Turbinado or raw cane sugar for topping

Preheat the oven to 400°F/200°C and grease a baking sheet. Cut the butter into ½-in/12-mm cubes and chill in the freezer for 15 minutes. In a medium bowl, mix together the kefir cream and leaven until well combined, then transfer to the freezer to chill. Wash, hull, and roughly chop the strawberries (if using raspberries or blueberries, wash them but leave whole), place in a bowl, and transfer to the freezer to chill.

In a large bowl, combine all three flours, the baking soda, baking powder, granulated sugar, 2 teaspoons of the salt, and the lemon zest, and whisk to combine. Spread the flour mixture out onto your work surface into a rectangle about ⅓ in/8 mm deep. Scatter the

chilled butter cubes over the flour. Toss a little of the flour over the butter so that your rolling pin won't stick, and then begin rolling the butter into the flour. When the butter starts flattening into long, thin pieces, use a bench scraper to scoop up the sides of the rectangle so that it is again the size you started with. Repeat the rolling and scraping three or four times.

Make a well in the center of the flour-butter mixture and pour all of the chilled kefir cream–leaven mixture into the well. Using the bench scraper, scoop the sides of the dough into the center, cutting the cream-leaven mixture into the dough as you work. Keep scraping and cutting until the dough is a shaggy mass, then shape the dough into a rectangle about 15 by 21 in/38 by 53 cm. Lightly dust the top with flour. Roll out the rectangle until it is the same dimensions as before, and then scrape the top, bottom, and sides together again. Transfer the dough to a baking sheet and chill in the refrigerator for 15 minutes. Roll out the rectangle to the same dimensions, add half of the berries, and then scrape the top, bottom, and sides together and chill in the refrigerator for 15 minutes. Roll out the rectangle once again to the same dimensions and add the remaining berries. Scrape the top, bottom, and sides together, and roll out until it is an 18-by-15-in/46-by-38-cm rectangle that's 1½ in/4 cm thick.

In a small bowl, beat together the egg and a pinch of salt. With a pastry brush, brush the egg wash over the surface of the dough and top generously with Turbinado sugar. Using a chef's knife, cut the dough into 12 triangles. Transfer the triangles to the prepared baking sheet, spacing them evenly, and chill in the refrigerator until firm, about 20 minutes.

Bake the scones until the tops are lightly browned, 25 to 35 minutes. Remove from the oven and serve warm.

Yield: Twelve scones

HAM & CHEESE SCONES

340 g/1½ cups cold unsalted butter

177 g/¾ cup Kefir Cultured Cream or Crème Fraîche (page 245)

170 g/¾ cup dry vermouth

170 g/¾ cup leaven (page 35)

142 g/5 oz smoked ham, cut into ¼-in/6-mm cubes

178 g/1½ cups grated Gruyère cheese

30 g/2 T freshly ground black pepper

30 g/2 T chopped mixed fresh herbs, such as thyme, marjoram, and parsley

341 g/2½ cups white pastry flour

204 g/1¾ cups oat flour

136 g/1 cup plus 1 T whole-wheat pastry flour

1 T baking powder

¾ t baking soda

1¼ t plus pinch of fine sea salt

50 g/1 large egg

Preheat the oven to 400°F/ 200°C and grease a baking sheet. Cut the butter into ½-in/12-mm cubes and chill in the freezer for 15 minutes. In a medium bowl, mix together the kefir cream, vermouth, and leaven until well combined, then transfer to the freezer to chill. In a medium bowl, combine the ham, Gruyère, black pepper, and fresh herbs and transfer to the freezer to chill.

In a large bowl combine all three flours, the baking powder, baking soda, the 1¼ teaspoons salt and whisk to combine. Spread the flour mixture out onto your work surface into a rectangle about ⅓ in/8 mm deep. Scatter the chilled butter cubes over the flour. Toss a little of the flour over the butter so that your rolling pin won't stick, and then begin rolling the butter into the flour. When the butter starts flattening into long, thin pieces, use a bench scraper to scoop up the sides of the rectangle so that it is again the size you started with. Repeat the rolling and scraping three or four times.

Make a well in the center of the flour-butter mixture and pour all of the chilled kefir cream–leaven mixture into the well. Using the bench scraper, scoop the sides of the dough onto the center, cutting the cream-leaven mixture into the dough as you work. Keep scraping and cutting until the dough is a shaggy mass, then shape the dough into a rectangle about 10 by 14 in/25 by 36 cm. Lightly dust the top with flour. Roll out the rectangle until it is 15 by 21 in/38 by 53 cm and then scrape the top, bottom, and sides together again to 10 by 14 in/25 by 36 cm. Transfer the dough to a baking sheet and chill in the refrigerator for 15 minutes. Remove the dough from the refrigerator. Add half the chilled ham and cheese mixture, roll out the rectangle once again until it is 15 by 21 in/38 by 53 cm and then scrape the top, bottom, and sides together to 10 by 14 in/25 by 36 cm. Add the remaining ham and cheese mixture and roll out the dough until it is half again as large, then scrape the top, bottom, and sides together and pat the dough out into an 18 by 5 in/46 by 12 cm rectangle that's 1½ in/4 cm thick.

In a small bowl, beat together the egg and a pinch of salt. With a pastry brush, brush the egg wash over the surface of the dough. Using a chef's knife, cut the dough into 12 triangles or rounds. Transfer the triangles to the prepared baking sheet, spacing them evenly, and chill in the refrigerator until firm, about 20 minutes.

Bake the scones for 25 to 35 minutes, until the tops are lightly browned. Remove from the oven and serve warm.

Yield: Twelve scones

BUCKWHEAT, BERGAMOT & BLOOD ORANGE CHIFFON CAKE

The idea here is to concentrate a few strong complementary flavors to create a cake that is pleasantly bitter and not too sweet. Tartine chiffon cake is made with whole-grain dark buckwheat flour, and then layered with blood orange marmalade and bergamot-infused blackout chocolate ganache. The ganache sets quickly, so cut your cake layers and have your filling and syrup on hand when ready to assemble.

BLOOD ORANGE MARMALADE FILLING

1 T lemon juice

1½ t powdered gelatin

170 g/½ cup blood orange marmalade

71 g/½ cup Candied Kumquats (see page 273), or other citrus peel in syrup

BUCKWHEAT CHIFFON CAKE

206 g/1½ cups whole-grain buckwheat flour

1¾ t baking powder

1 t fine sea salt

124 g/½ cup plus 2 T superfine sugar

114 g/½ cup whole milk

65 g/3 egg yolks

56 g/¼ cup grapeseed oil

37 g/2 T plus 1 t water

289 g/10 egg whites

¼ t cream of tartar or lemon juice

BERGAMOT SYRUP

114 g/½ cup water

100 g/½ cup sugar

114 g/½ cup bergamot or blood orange juice

EARL GREY CRÈME ANGLAISE GANACHE

220 g/1⅓ cups chopped bittersweet chocolate (70%), preferably Valrhona

6 g/2 T loose-leaf Earl Grey tea (or 4 tea bags) steeped overnight in 220 g/1 cup cold heavy cream

220 g/1 cup whole milk

86 g/4 egg yolks, at room temperature

42 g/3 T sugar

Cocoa powder for dusting

To make the filling: Pour the lemon juice into a medium nonreactive bowl and add the gelatin. Stir to dissolve the gelatin, then add the marmalade and the candied citrus. Refrigerate until cool and set, about 2 hours (this can be made and refrigerated up to a day ahead).

To make the cake: Preheat the oven to 325°F/165°C. Line the bottom of 10-in/25-cm springform cake pan with parchment paper and set aside.

Sift together the flour, baking powder, and salt into a large bowl. Add 100 g/½ cup of the sugar and whisk to combine.

In a medium bowl, whisk together the milk, egg yolks, oil, and water. Make a well in the flour, add the yolk mixture, then whisk thoroughly and quickly for about 1 minute until very smooth.

Put the egg whites in the bowl of a stand mixer fitted with the whisk attachment. Beat on medium speed until frothy. Add the cream of tartar and beat on medium-high speed until the whites hold soft peaks. Slowly add

the remaining 24 g/2 tablespoons sugar and beat on medium-high speed until the whites hold firm, shiny peaks. Using a rubber spatula, scoop about one-third of the whites into the bowl containing the batter and, with the rubber spatula, gently fold in to lighten the batter. Gently fold the remaining whites into the batter just until combined.

Pour the batter into the prepared pan, smoothing the top with an offset spatula. Bake until a cake tester inserted into the center comes out clean, about 1 hour and 15 minutes. Let cool in the pan on a wire rack. To unmold, run a paring knife around the inside of the pan to loosen the cake, release and remove the outside ring of the pan, then invert the cake onto the wire rack and peel off the parchment. (The cake will keep, tightly wrapped, in the refrigerator for up to 4 days or in the freezer for up to 1 month.)

To make the syrup: In a medium saucepan over medium heat combine the water, sugar, and bergamot juice and bring to a simmer. Simmer, stirring occasionally, until the sugar dissolves. Remove from the heat and let cool completely.

Wash, dry, and reassemble the springform pan. With a long, thin, serrated knife, cut the cake lengthwise into five equal layers. Place one layer in the bottom of the springform pan.

To make the ganache: Place a saucepan of water over medium heat and bring to a simmer. Set a heatproof bowl over the water, taking care that the bottom of the bowl does not touch the water. Add the chocolate and heat until halfway melted. Stir gently, remove from the heat, and let cool until it registers between 95°F/35°C and 115°F/46°C on an instant-read thermometer.

Remove the tea-infused cream from the refrigerator and strain through a fine-mesh sieve into a separate medium saucepan (if using tea bags, simply discard them). Add the milk and place over medium heat. Heat until it comes to just a boil, stirring occasionally.

In a separate bowl, whisk together the egg yolks and sugar. Whisking constantly, pour one-third of the hot cream mixture into the yolk-sugar mixture, then add this mixture to the remaining cream. Stir constantly over medium heat with a wooden spoon until the mixture thickens and coats the back of a spoon. Remove from the heat and pour through a fine-mesh sieve into a clean bowl and let it cool until it registers 140°F/60°C on an instant-read thermometer. This is your crème Anglaise.

Measure out 600 g/2¼ cups crème Anglaise and add to the chocolate in four or five additions, using a heatproof spatula and vigorous strokes to incorporate. The temperature of the mixture should not exceed 113°F/43°C, which is why the cream is added in several additions. The mixture may appear broken at first but should come together by the final addition of cream to be smooth and glossy. Let cool slightly. With a handheld immersion blender, blend the ganache until completely smooth and uniform. (A whisk is also fine, but an immersion blender makes for an ultra-silky ganache that pours very nicely.) Use immediately.

Using a pastry brush, soak the cake layer in the pan with one-quarter of the bergamot syrup. With an offset spatula, spread a thin layer of ganache (about ¼ in/6 mm thick) over the cake. Top with a second cake layer, soak with an additional one-quarter of berga-mot syrup, and then spread with half of the marmalade filling. Top with a third layer and repeat the process, alternating with one more layer of ganache and one more layer of marmalade filling, soaking each cake layer well with syrup. Top with the final cake layer, soak with the remaining syrup, and refrigerate until the cake is firm, 1 to 2 hours, then dust with cocoa powder.

Remove the cake from the refrigerator 2 hours before serving to bring to room tem-perature. To store, cover tightly and keep in a cool place for up to 4 days.

Yield: One 10-in/25-cm cake

BOHEMIAN APPLE LAYER CAKE

This moist home-style layer cake contains a handful of my favorite autumn ingredients. The cake is made with Kamut flour; sweetened with prunes and raisins; spiced with cinnamon, cloves, and nutmeg; and layered with apple butter and prune compote. The whole is finished with a frosting made of cider reduced with rye whiskey.

APPLE CAKE

391 g/2¾ cups whole-grain Kamut flour

24 g/2 T plus 2 t unsweetened cocoa powder

¾ t baking soda

¾ t fine sea salt

¾ t ground cinnamon

¾ t ground cloves

¾ t ground nutmeg

¾ t ground allspice

150 g/⅔ cup unsalted butter, at room temperature

300 g/1½ cups granulated sugar

150 g/3 large eggs, room temperature

488 g/2 cups applesauce

224 g/1½ cups finely chopped pitted prunes

149 g/1 cup golden raisins

114 g/1 cup finely chopped walnuts

340 g/3 cups firm, tart apples (such as Gravenstein or Granny Smith), peeled, cored, and diced into large chunks

PRUNE COMPOTE

378 g/3⅓ cups pitted prunes

228 g/1 cup Pinot Noir or other light-bodied red wine

76 g/⅓ cup brandy

37 g/3 T granulated sugar

1 vanilla bean, halved and seeds scraped

1 cinnamon stick

Peel of 1 orange

675 g/3 cups apple butter, homemade or store-bought

CIDER FROSTING

456 g/2 cups apple cider

114 g/½ cup rye whiskey

1 cinnamon stick

1 clove

50 g/¼ cup granulated sugar

228 g/1 cup unsalted butter, at room temperature

114 g/⅔ cup chopped white chocolate, melted and cooled

114 g/1 cup walnuts, toasted and chopped

To make the cake: Grease a 10-in/25-cm round cake pan and dust with flour. Preheat the oven to 350°F/180°C. Sift together the flour, cocoa powder, baking soda, salt, cinnamon, cloves, nutmeg, and allspice into a medium bowl. In the bowl of a stand mixer fitted with the paddle attachment, beat the butter and sugar on medium speed until well combined, about 2 minutes. Add the eggs, one at a time, scraping down the bowl after each addition.

Reduce the mixer speed to medium-low and add the flour mixture in three additions, alternating with the applesauce, and scraping down the bowl after each addition. With a rubber spatula, fold in the prunes, raisins, walnuts, and apples.

Transfer the batter to the prepared pan, smoothing the top, and bake for 1 hour, until the cake springs back when touched and a cake tester inserted into the center comes out clean. Transfer to a wire rack and let cool for 1 hour, then run a thin knife around the edge of the pan and unmold the cake onto a wire rack.

To make the compote: In a medium, heavy-bottomed saucepan over medium-high heat, combine the prunes, wine, brandy, sugar, vanilla bean and seeds, cinnamon stick, and orange peel and cook, stirring occasionally, until the mixture boils. Reduce to a simmer and cook until the prunes are soft and the liquid is reduced by half, about 30 minutes. Let cool, then transfer to a food processor and process into a thick paste. (The compote can be stored in the refrigerator up to 2 weeks.)

With a long serrated knife, cut the cake lengthwise into four equal layers. Place one layer on a plate or cake stand. With an offset spatula, spread one-third of the prune compote over the cake, then top with 225 g/1 cup apple butter, spreading evenly. Top with a second cake layer and spread with half the remaining compote and 225 g/1 cup of apple butter. Add a third layer, topping with the remaining compote and apple butter. Top with the final cake layer and refrigerate for 1 hour.

To make the frosting: In a small saucepan over medium-high heat, combine the cider, whiskey, cinnamon stick, and clove. When the liquid is hot, whisk in the sugar until dissolved, then lower the heat to medium and continue simmering until the liquid has reduced to 60 g/ ¼ cup; it will be thick and syrupy. Remove the clove and cinnamon stick and let cool to room temperature. (The syrup can be stored in the refrigerator for up to 1 week.)

In a stand mixer fitted with the paddle attachment, beat the butter on medium-high speed until soft and creamy. Beat in the white chocolate. Add the cider syrup and beat until combined.

With an offset spatula, frost the cake with a very thin layer of frosting. Return the cake to the refrigerator and let chill for 30 minutes. Finish the cake with the remaining frosting and pat the sides of the cake with the chopped walnuts, pressing to adhere.

Remove the cake from the refrigerator 2 hours before serving to bring to room temperature. The cake will keep, refrigerated, for up to 4 days.

Yield: One 10-in/25-cm layer cake

CHOCOLATE-RYE ROULADE

This roulade cake is based on the classic Tartine biscuit recipe, but uses whole-grain dark rye flour in place of the pastry flour. Cocoa powder is used to flavor and color the cake. The mousse filling, made with mascarpone and flavored with candied citrus peel and cocoa nibs, is loosely based on a cannoli-inspired tart filling we make at the bakery.

CHOCOLATE-RYE CAKE
114 g/1 cup whole-grain dark rye flour
57 g/⅔ cup unsweetened cocoa powder
350 g/7 large eggs, at room temperature
170 g/¾ cup plus 2 T superfine sugar
Pinch of fine sea salt
28 g/2 T unsalted butter, melted

COFFEE-RUM SYRUP
114 g/½ cup brewed coffee
60 g/¼ cup dark rum
60 g /¼ cup water
51 g/¼ cup granulated sugar

MASCARPONE MOUSSE
60 g/¼ cup water
51 g/¼ cup granulated sugar
40 g/2 T plus 2 t sweet marsala wine
20 g/1 T plus 1 t dark rum
20 g/1 T plus 1 t fresh lemon juice
1½ t powdered gelatin

215 g/1 cup mascarpone

600 g/2⅔ cups heavy cream

200 g/¾ cup plus 2 T Kefir Cultured Cream or Crème Fraîche (page 245)

¼ t fine sea salt

60 g/⅓ cup superfine sugar

2 t vanilla extract

200 g/1 cup finely diced Candied Kumquats (page 273) or orange peel

180 g/1½ cups cocoa nibs

CHOCOLATE GANACHE

228 g/1⅓ cups chopped dark chocolate (70%), preferably Valrhona

220 g/1 cup heavy cream

Cocoa nibs for decorating

Powdered sugar for decorating

To make the cake: Preheat the oven to 350°F/ 180°C. Line an 11-by-17-in/28-by-43-cm baking sheet with parchment paper and set aside. Sift together the flour and cocoa powder into a medium bowl and set aside.

In the bowl of a stand mixer fitted with the whisk attachment, beat together the eggs, superfine sugar, and salt on low speed until just combined. Place a saucepan of water over medium heat and bring to a simmer. Set the mixer bowl over the water, taking care that the bottom of the bowl does not touch the water. Continue to whisk until the mixture is hot to the touch (it should register 120°F/48°C on an instant-read thermometer), 5 to 7 minutes.

Return the bowl to the mixer stand. Beat on medium-high speed until pale yellow, tripled in volume, and the egg mixture falls from the whisk in a wide ribbon that folds back on itself and slowly dissolves on the surface, 3 to 5 minutes. Using a rubber spatula, gently but thoroughly fold in the flour mixture in three additions. Transfer one-quarter of the batter to a separate bowl and whisk in the melted butter, then gently but quickly fold back into the rest of the batter, taking care not to overmix and deflate the batter.

Pour the batter into the center of the prepared baking sheet, mixing in any flour clumps that remain in the bowl as you pour. Using an offset spatula, gently guide the batter to the four corners of the baking sheet and smooth out the surface so you have an even layer of batter.

Bake for 10 to 15 minutes, rotating the pan halfway through baking, until the top springs back when lightly touched. Remove from the oven and let cool in the baking sheet on a wire rack. To unmold, run a paring knife around the edges of the baking sheet to loosen the cake and then release by using an offset spatula to lift one side; the cake will lift up, attached to the parchment paper, in one piece. Invert the cake onto a clean surface, peel off the parchment, and then proceed with the assembly. (The cake will keep, tightly wrapped, in the refrigerator for up to 3 days or in the freezer for up to 1 month.)

To make the coffee-rum syrup: In a small saucepan over medium heat, combine the coffee, rum, water, and granulated sugar. Bring to a simmer and cook, stirring, just until the sugar dissolves, then remove from heat and let cool completely.

To make the mascarpone mousse: In a small saucepan over medium heat, combine the water, granulated sugar, marsala, rum, and lemon juice. Bring to a simmer and cook, stirring, just until the sugar dissolves. Remove from the heat, transfer to a large bowl, and let cool until just warm to the touch. Scatter the gelatin over the mixture and let stand for 5 minutes.

In the bowl of a stand mixer fitted with the paddle attachment, beat together the mascarpone, 150 g/⅔ cup of the heavy cream, the kefir cream, and salt on low speed until smooth. Transfer to a clean bowl and put in the refrigerator.

To the now-empty mixer bowl, add the remaining cream, superfine sugar, and vanilla and beat on medium-high speed until soft peaks form. Transfer to the refrigerator.

Whisk the marsala-rum mixture into the mascarpone mixture. Keep whisking until you have a very smooth mixture, then switch to a spatula and fold in the whipped cream. Fold in the candied orange peel and cocoa nibs.

On a clean work surface, arrange an 11-by-17-in/28-by-43-cm piece of parchment paper or two overlapping sheets of plastic wrap with the long side facing you and place the cake on top with the long side facing you.

Using a pastry brush, moisten the cake with the coffee-rum syrup, working in quadrants to ensure that the cake gets soaked evenly. You can press lightly with your fingers to locate spots of the cake that need more soaking; use all of the syrup.

With an offset spatula, spread the mascarpone mousse onto the cake, leaving a 1-in/2.5-cm margin on the two long sides of the cake. Starting from the long side nearest you, begin rolling up the cake, using the parchment to help you lift and roll evenly and tightly. Rotate the cake so the seam side is facing down, then transfer to a baking sheet (with the plastic supporting it) and refrigerate the rolled cake until the mousse is firm, at least 2 hours or up to overnight.

To prepare the ganache: Place a saucepan of water over medium heat and bring to a simmer. Set a heatproof bowl over the water, taking care that the bottom of the bowl does not touch the water. Add the chocolate and heat until halfway melted. Stir gently, remove from the heat, and let cool until it registers between 95°F/35°C and 115°F/46°C on an instant-read thermometer.

In a separate medium saucepan over medium-high heat, bring the cream to just under a boil; do not let the temperature of the cream exceed 140°F/60°C. Add the hot cream to the chocolate in four or five additions, using a heatproof spatula and vigorous strokes to incorporate. The temperature of the mixture should not exceed 113°F/43°C, which is why the cream is added in several additions. The mixture may appear broken at first but should come together by the final addition of cream to be smooth and glossy. Let cool slightly. With a handheld immersion blender, blend the ganache until completely smooth and uniform. Use immediately.

Set a wire rack on top of a large, baking sheet. Set the chilled cake on the rack and pour the ganache over the cake, allowing the excess to drip off and collect in the baking sheet. When still wet, finish with a line of cocoa nibs and a thin dusting of powdered sugar. Transfer the cake (still on the rack set over the baking sheet) to the refrigerator and refrigerate until the ganache is set, about 30 minutes.

Remove the cake from the fridge and, using a sharp serrated knife, cut off the ends of the cake on a diagonal to make a neater presentation. Transfer the cake to a platter and serve.

Yield: One 17-in/43-cm long roulade

CHOCOLATE-RYE TART

A traditional Hungarian sweet, this is a dark rye and cocoa short crust filled with chocolate-studded meringue and baked. Alternatively, the crust can be filled with frangipane (see page 325) and topped with fresh cherries or apricots before baking. The dough used to form the crust can also be blind baked and filled with honey-lemon cream (see page 251) and berries.

CHOCOLATE-RYE DOUGH

500 g/2 cups plus 2 T unsalted butter, at room temperature

200 g/1 cup granulated sugar

50 g/1 large egg, at room temperature

20 g/1 egg yolk, at room temperature

½ t vanilla extract

284 g/2⅓ cups rye flour, sifted

171 g/2 cups unsweetened cocoa powder, sifted, plus more for dusting

CHOCOLATE MERINGUE FILLING

120 g/4 egg whites

200 g/1 cup granulated sugar

50 g/⅓ cup blanched almonds

½ vanilla bean, cut into 3 pieces

114 g/⅔ cup grated unsweetened chocolate, preferably Valrhona

85 g/¼ cup apricot jam

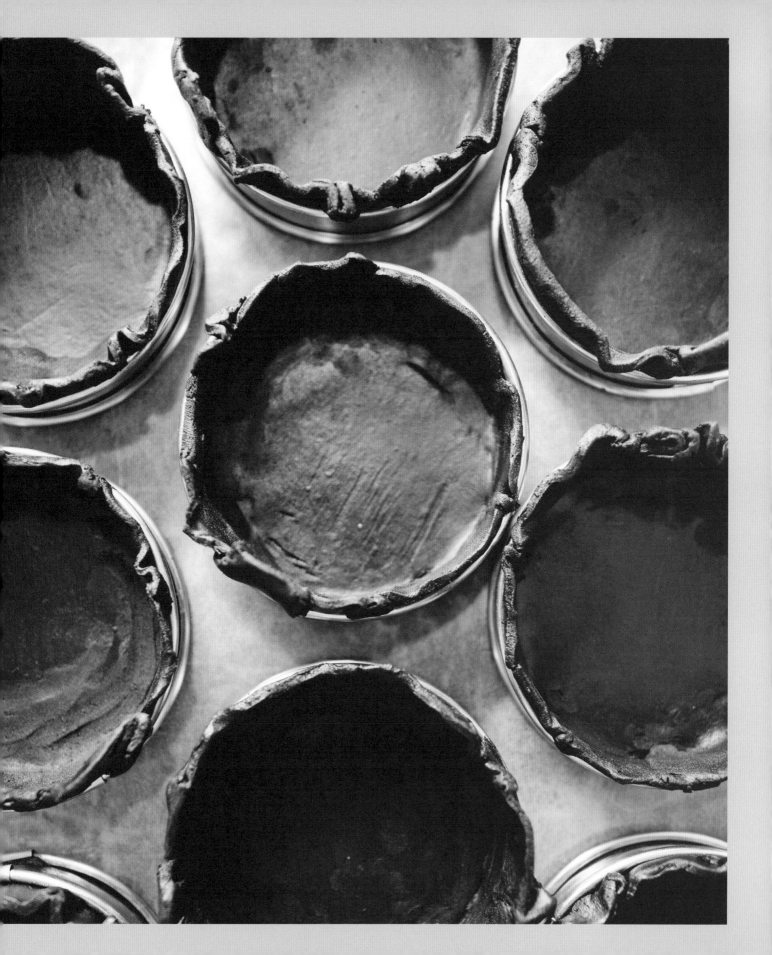

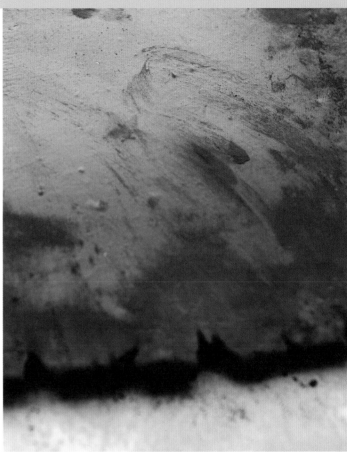

EGG WASH
  20 g/1 egg yolk
  30 g/2 T heavy cream

To make the dough: In the bowl of a stand mixer fitted with the paddle attachment, beat together the butter and sugar on medium speed until creamy but not voluminous, 1 to 2 minutes. Add the egg and mix to combine, then add the egg yolk. Stop the mixer and scrape down the sides of the bowl with a rubber spatula. Turn the mixer to low speed, add the vanilla, and mix to combine. Add the flour and cocoa and mix until combined. Transfer the dough to a large piece of plastic wrap, pat into a rectangle, wrap tightly, and refrigerate until firm, at least 1 hour.

Divide the chilled dough into two equal pieces; rewrap one piece and return it to the refrigerator. Dust both sides of one piece of dough lightly with cocoa powder, transfer to a sheet of parchment paper or plastic wrap, and cover with a second sheet of parchment paper or plastic wrap. Roll out the dough between the parchment or plastic wrap, rotating the dough periodically to ensure an even thickness of about ⅛ in/4 mm and a diameter of 14 in/36 cm. Transfer the dough to the refrigerator (still sandwiched between the parchment) and let chill while you roll the second piece of dough, using the same technique.

While the second piece of dough is chilling, remove the first round and gently ease the dough into a 9-in/23-cm tart pan with a removable bottom, rotating and lightly pressing to ensure that the dough adheres to the side of the pan. With a sharp knife, trim the dough level with the top of the pan. Discard any excess dough. Place the tart shell in the freezer until firm, about 15 minutes.

Preheat the oven to 350°F/180°C. Remove the second pastry round from the fridge and, with a pastry wheel or pizza cutter, cut the dough into ¾-in/2-cm strips. Return the strips to the refrigerator.

Line the tart shell with a piece of parchment paper and fill with pie weights. Bake for 15 to 20 minutes, until slightly puffy and matte. Remove from the oven, remove the pie weights, and let cool to room temperature, then refrigerate while you prepare the filling. Increase the oven temperature to 400°F/200°C.

To make the meringue filling: In the bowl of a stand mixer fitted with the whisk attachment, whip the egg whites on medium-high speed until foamy, then add the sugar a little at a time until fully incorporated. Turn the mixer to high and beat the egg whites until stiff peaks form, 3 to 5 minutes.

Place the almonds and vanilla bean in the bowl of a food processor and pulse until the mixture has the texture of coarse meal. Gently fold the almond mixture into the beaten egg whites, then fold in the chocolate.

Spread the bottom of the baked tart shell with the apricot jam, then fill with the meringue, using an offset spatula to smooth it in an even, flat layer. Remove the strips of dough from the refrigerator and arrange half of the dough strips atop the meringue, spacing evenly. Form a lattice by placing the remaining dough strips in the opposite direction atop the filling. Trim the ends of the dough strips even with the edge, pressing to seal.

To make the egg wash: In a small bowl, whisk together the egg yolk and heavy cream.

Brush the lattice strips and the edge of the tart with the egg wash. Bake for 30 minutes, until the meringue puffs and darkens slightly in color. If you notice the meringue coloring too quickly, reduce the oven temperature to 375°F/190°C, rotate your tart, and continue to bake.

Let cool completely to room temperature before slicing. Store for up to 2 days at room temperature.

Yield: One 9-in/23-cm lattice-topped tart

BUCKWHEAT-APPLE TART

For this gluten-free tart, the short dough used to make the crust is made with whole-grain buckwheat flour, egg yolks, and butter. The filling, comprises grated apples bound with chopped walnuts, makes a striking contrast to the black pastry.

BUCKWHEAT TART DOUGH

298 g/1 cup plus 5 T cold unsalted butter

312 g/2⅓ cups whole-grain buckwheat flour

192 g/1 cup sucanat

2 t fine sea salt

1 t cornstarch

80 g/4 egg yolks, at room temperature

20 g/1 T plus 1 t Crème Fraîche or Kefir Cultured Cream (page 245)

APPLE FILLING

48 g/½ cup walnuts

454 g/7 to 8 firm, tart apples (such as Gravenstein, Jonathan, or Granny Smith), peeled, cored, and coarsely grated

1 T fresh lemon juice

1 T whole-grain buckwheat flour

1 T cornstarch

48 g/3 T plus 1 t unsalted butter, melted

65 g/⅓ cup granulated sugar

½ vanilla bean, split lengthwise and seeds scraped

43 g/¼ cup packed golden raisins, soaked in hot water for 10 minutes, then drained

EGG WASH

20 g/1 egg yolk

30 g/2 T heavy cream

Turbinado or Demerara sugar for topping

To make the buckwheat tart dough: Cut the butter into 1-in/2.5-cm cubes and chill in the freezer for 15 minutes.

Measure the flour onto your work surface. Spread the flour out into a rectangle about ⅓ in/8 mm deep. Scatter the butter cubes over the flour. Toss a little of the flour over the butter so that your rolling pin won't stick and then begin rolling. When the butter starts flattening out into long, thin pieces, use a bench scraper to scoop up the sides of the rectangle so that it is again the size you started with. Repeat the rolling and scraping three or four times—the dough will be a shaggy pile with visible long ribbons of butter throughout.

In a medium bowl, whisk together the sucanat, salt, and cornstarch. Beat in the egg yolks, one at a time, then whisk in the crème fraîche until thoroughly combined. Scrape the flour-butter mixture together into a mound, make a well in the center, and pour the egg mixture into the well. Using the bench scraper, scoop the sides of the dough onto the center, cutting the crème fraîche mixture into the dough.

Keep scraping and cutting until the dough is a shaggy mass, then shape the dough into a 10-by-14-in/25-by-36-cm rectangle. Lightly dust the top with flour. Roll out the rectangle until it is half again as large and then scrape the top, bottom, and sides together and reroll. Repeat three or four times until you have a smooth and cohesive dough. You should have a neat rectangle measuring about 10 by 14 in/25 by 36 cm. Transfer the dough to a large baking sheet, cover with plastic, and refrigerate for about 1 hour.

To make the apple filling: Preheat the oven to 350°F/180°C. Spread the walnuts in a single layer on a baking sheet and toast until golden brown, about 7 minutes. Remove from the oven and allow to cool, then finely chop.

In a large bowl, toss together the apples and lemon juice. Stir in the walnuts, flour, cornstarch, butter, sugar, vanilla bean seeds, and golden raisins and mix until well combined.

Divide the chilled dough into two equal portions. To roll a circle from what is roughly a square, start out with the dough positioned as a diamond in front of you, with the ends of the rolling pin parallel to two points of the square. Roll from the center toward each end, flattening only the center, not the two points that are nearest to and farthest from you (at top and bottom); leave those two points thick. Now turn the dough so that the flattened-out corners are at the top and bottom. Again, roll

from the center toward the points nearest to and farthest from you, again stopping short of both the top and bottom. Now you should have a square that has little humps in between the pointy corners. Roll out the thicker areas and you will begin to see a circle forming.

Keep rolling until the dough is a little more than ⅛ in/4 mm thick (each circle should be about 14 in/35 cm in diameter). Transfer the circles to a baking sheet using your rolling pin, placing parchment between the layers. Refrigerate until firm, about 10 minutes.

Fit one circle of dough into the bottom of a 9-in/23-cm removable-bottom tart pan, folding in the sides to ensure that the dough is not stretched to fit the shell but instead meets all the curves of the pan. Add the apple filling, smoothing it out so that the tart is full to the brim but not mounded. Lay the second round of dough on top of the filling, pressing from the center out to expel excess air and pinching down on the edges to adhere the top dough to the bottom, then crimp. Refrigerate until firm, about 10 minutes. Increase the oven temperature to 400°F/200°C.

To make the egg wash: In a small bowl, whisk together the egg yolk and heavy cream.

Brush the egg wash over the tart and top with the Turbinado sugar. You can bake the tart immediately or refrigerate it, unwrapped, for up to 2 hours. (Or you can skip the egg wash and sugar, wrap the tart tightly, and freeze it for up to 2 weeks. When ready to bake, remove from the freezer, brush with the egg wash, top with sugar, and bake straightaway, increasing the baking time by 10 minutes.)

Bake the tart for about 30 minutes until the crust has visibly puffed and baked to a dark blue/brown color, rotating the tart halfway through baking to ensure even browning. If the pastry is browning too quickly, reduce the oven temperature to 375°F/190°C or tent the tart loosely with aluminum foil. Remove from the oven and let cool to room temperature on a wire rack. Serve warm or at room temperature. Store for up to 2 days at room temperature.

Yield: One double-crust 9-in/23-cm apple tart, serves 8 to 12

BUCKWHEAT TART WITH HONEY-LEMON CREAM

Based on the classic "tarte citron" that Liz learned to make when we were living and baking in Provence, the crust here is made of whole-grain buckwheat pâte sucrée and filled with lemon cream sweetened with buckwheat honey. The finished tart can be topped with fresh berries.

BUCKWHEAT PÂTE SUCRÉE

114 g/½ cup unsalted butter, at room temperature

75 g/¼ cup plus 2 T granulated sugar

30 g/¼ cup powdered sugar, sifted

20 g/1 egg yolk

160 g/¾ cup plus 2 T whole-grain buckwheat flour

¼ t fine sea salt

HONEY-LEMON CREAM

148 g/½ cup plus 2 T fresh lemon juice

200 g/4 large eggs

57 g/¼ cup granulated sugar

57 g/3 T buckwheat honey

227 g/1 cup unsalted butter, at room temperature

EGG WASH

29 g/1 egg white

Pinch of fine sea salt

2 T heavy cream

228 g/1 cup heavy cream

To make the pâte sucrée: In the bowl of a stand mixer fitted with the paddle attachment, combine the butter and both sugars and mix on medium speed until smooth. Add the egg yolk, mixing to combine, then scrape down the bowl with a rubber spatula. Add the flour and salt all at once and mix on low speed until just incorporated. Scrape down the sides of the bowl, divide the dough into two balls, shape each ball into a disk, then wrap in plastic. Refrigerate one disk of dough for at least 2 hours, or up to overnight; transfer the other disk to the freezer for future use. (It will keep for 1 month.)

To make the honey-lemon cream: Place a fine-mesh sieve over a medium bowl and set within easy reach. Bring a saucepan of water to a simmer over medium-high heat. In a heatproof bowl that fits securely on top of the saucepan, combine the lemon juice, eggs, granulated sugar, and honey, and whisk to combine. Place a saucepan of water over medium heat and bring to a simmer. Set the bowl over the water, taking care that the bottom of the bowl does not touch the water, and cook, whisking constantly, until

the mixture becomes very thick and registers 175°F/80°C on an instant-read thermometer, 8 to 10 minutes. Remove from the heat and pour the mixture through the fine-mesh sieve into the bowl. Let cool to 140°F/60°C, stirring occasionally to prevent a skin from forming.

Cut the butter into small pieces. When the honey-lemon cream is at 140°F/60°C, add the butter, one piece at a time, whisking after each addition until incorporated. The mixture will be pale yellow, opaque, and quite thick. (You can use the cream immediately, or refrigerate it for up to 5 days in an airtight container.)

Place the chilled dough on a lightly floured surface and roll out to a thickness of ⅛ in/4 mm and a diameter of 11 in/28 cm, rolling from the center toward the edge in all directions. Lift and rotate the dough a quarter turn after every few strokes, dusting the work surface with flour as necessary to discourage sticking and working quickly to prevent the dough from becoming warm. (If the dough has become too soft to work with, put it in the refrigerator for a few minutes to firm up before transferring it to the pan.) Carefully transfer the dough to a 9-in/23-cm fluted tart pan with a removable bottom, easing it into the bottom and sides and then pressing gently into place. Do not stretch the dough or the sides will shrink during baking. If the dough develops any tears, patch with a little extra dough and press firmly to adhere. With a sharp knife, trim the dough level with the top of the pan. Discard any excess dough. Place the pastry shell in the refrigerator or freezer until firm, about 15 minutes.

Preheat the oven to 350°F/180°C. Bake the shell for 10 minutes, then rotate the pan and continue baking for 5 to 10 minutes, until dark blue-purple around the edges.

To make the egg wash: In a small bowl, whisk together the egg white, salt, and cream. Brush the tart shell on the bottom and edges with the egg wash, then return it to the oven for 1 to 2 minutes. Remove from the oven, transfer to a wire rack, and let cool to room temperature before filling.

Pour the honey-lemon cream into the shell. Refrigerate until firm, about 1 hour.

In a stand mixer fitted with the whisk attachment, beat the heavy cream until it holds soft peaks. Top the tart with the whipped cream and serve.

Yield: One 9-in/23-cm tart or
six 4-in/10-cm tarts

CHERRY GALETTES

Liz and I were first introduced to Kamut—an ancient durum wheat—by Dave Miller when we helped open his bakery in the foothills of the Sierra Nevada in 1994. Dave was already milling his own bio-dynamically grown grains, and using a wide range of seeds and grains in his bread, many of them grown for him by legendary sustainable farm movement leader Fred Kirschenmann in North Dakota.

Dave's challenge to Liz at the time was for her to make pastries using whole grains, vegan if possible. The first recipe Liz developed using Kamut was a carrot tea cake. Since then, we've found this grain to be exceptionally versatile, working well in both bread and pastry while adding its distinct character to each. Applying the basic Tartine galette technique using Kamut flour and replacing the water with kefir cultured cream yields an extremely tender and flaky crust with a rich depth of flavor.

DOUGH
455 g/2 cups unsalted butter, very cold

250 g/1 cup Kefir Cultured Cream or Crème Fraîche (page 245)

1½ t fine sea salt

680 g/4¾ cups whole-grain Kamut flour

FILLING
1361 g/6 cups sweet cherries, pitted

Juice of 1 lemon

50 g/¼ cup granulated sugar

EGG WASH
20 g/1 egg yolk

30 g/2 T heavy cream

Turbinado or Demerara sugar

To make the dough: Cut the butter into 1-in/2.5-cm cubes and chill in the freezer for 10 minutes. Combine the kefir cream and salt in a small bowl and freeze for 10 minutes.

Spread the flour out onto your work surface into a rectangle about ⅓ in/8 mm deep. Scatter the chilled butter cubes over the flour. Toss a little of the flour over the butter so that your rolling pin won't stick, and then begin rolling the butter into the flour. When the butter starts flattening into long, thin pieces, use a bench scraper to scoop up the sides of the rectangle so that it is again the size you started with. Repeat the rolling and scraping three or four times; the dough will be a shaggy pile with visible ribbons of butter throughout.

Make a well in the center of the dry ingredients and pour all of the chilled kefir cream into the well. Using the bench scraper, scoop the sides of the dough onto the center, cutting the cultured cream into the dough. Keep scraping and cutting until the dough is a shaggy mass, then shape the dough into a rectangle about 10 by 14 in/25 by 36 cm. Lightly dust the top with flour. Roll out the rectangle until it is half again as large, then scrape the top, bottom, and sides together to the original size and reroll. Repeat three or four times until you have a smooth, cohesive dough. You should have a neat rectangle measuring about 10 by 14 in/25 by 36 cm. Transfer the dough to a large baking sheet, cover with plastic wrap, and refrigerate for about 1 hour.

To make the fruit filling: In a large bowl, combine the cherries and lemon juice. Set aside.

Divide the dough into two equal portions if making large galettes or twelve equal portions if making small galettes. To roll a circle from what is roughly a square, start with the dough positioned as a diamond in front of you, with the ends of the rolling pin parallel to two points of the square. Roll from the center toward each end, only flattening the center, not the two points that are nearest to and farthest from you (at top and bottom); leave those two points thick. Now turn the dough so that the flattened-out corners are at the top and bottom. Again, roll from the center toward the points nearest to and farthest from you, again stopping short of both the top and bottom. Now you should have a square that has little humps between the pointy corners. Roll out the thicker areas and you will begin to see a circle form.

Keep rolling until the dough is a little more than ⅛ in/4 mm thick for large galettes (each circle should be about 14 in/35 cm in diameter) and a little thinner for individual galettes (each circle should be 6 to 7 in/15 to 17 cm in diameter). Fold the large circles into quarters, transfer each one to a baking sheet, and unfold. Transfer the small circles to baking sheets without folding. Refrigerate the circles until firm, about 10 minutes.

Fill the center of each dough circle with some of the cherries, leaving a 2-in/5-cm border uncovered on the large galettes and a 1-in/2.5-cm border uncovered on the small galettes. Fold in the sides of the circles to partially cover the fruit, being sure not to leave any valleys where the fruit juice can leak out. Add 25 g/2 tablespoons of the granulated sugar over the fruit for each large tart and 1 teaspoon of sugar for each small tart. Refrigerate until firm, about 10 minutes. While the galettes are chilling, preheat the oven to 375°F/190°C.

To make the egg wash: In a small bowl, whisk together the egg yolk and heavy cream.

Brush the egg wash over the pastry edges, then top the pastry with the Turbinado sugar.

You can bake the galettes immediately or, dividing them evenly, refrigerate, unwrapped, for up to 2 hours. (Or you can skip the egg wash and sugar, wrap the galettes airtight, and freeze them for up to 2 weeks. When ready to bake, remove from the freezer, brush with the egg wash and dust with Turbinado sugar, and bake straightaway. Add 10 minutes to the baking time.)

Bake the galettes until the crust has visibly puffed and baked to a dark brown and the juice from the fruit is bubbling, 45 to 60 minutes for large galettes and 40 to 50 minutes for small galettes. Rotate and switch the baking sheets between the racks halfway through baking. If the pastry is browning too quickly, reduce the oven temperature to 350°F/180°C or place aluminum foil over the tops of the galettes. Remove from the oven and serve hot, or let cool on a wire rack and serve warm or at room temperature. Galettes will keep at room temperature for up to 2 days.

Yield: Two 12-in/30-cm or
twelve 4-in/10-cm galettes

INVERTED SPELT PUFF PASTRY DOUGH

Making puff pastry using high-extraction flour required a lot of testing to arrive at a recipe that gave us the exceptional flakiness expected in the classic mille-feuille. The inside-out technique— basically enveloping the dough inside of the butter rather than enveloping the butter inside laminating the dough — always requires careful precision; using high-extraction spelt flour renders the already delicate dough slightly more so. But the results are worth the effort: a whole-grain puff pastry that is every bit as delicate and flaky as its white-flour counterpart, if slightly more hearty.

200 g/¾ cup plus 2 T cold water

½ t white vinegar

1 T plus 1 t fine sea salt

667 g/3⅔ cups spelt flour, plus more for dusting

150 g/½ cup plus 2 T unsalted butter, melted and cooled

500 g/2 cups plus 3 T unsalted butter, at room temperature

In a measuring cup, combine the water, vinegar, and salt. Stir to dissolve and transfer to the refrigerator or freezer until very cold, about 30 minutes.

In the bowl of a stand mixer fitted with the dough hook, place 467 g/3⅓ cups of the spelt flour. Mix on low speed while slowly but steadily adding in the melted butter in a stream around the perimeter of the bowl.

When all the melted butter has been incorporated, steadily add in the chilled water mixture around the perimeter of the bowl. Let the dough mix on medium-low speed until it comes together, then continue to mix until the dough is smooth and a bit shiny, 3 to 5 minutes longer.

Transfer the dough to a parchment-lined baking sheet, pat into a 4-by-6-in/10-by-15-cm rectangle, and refrigerate until very cold, but no longer than 1 hour.

In the bowl of the stand mixer fitted with the paddle attachment, combine the remaining 200 g/⅓ cup spelt flour and the room-temperature butter on low speed for 1 to 2 minutes, until it becomes a smooth, cohesive mass. You do not want to add volume to the butter, so do not turn the speed up any higher than low. Turn the mixture out onto a parchment-lined baking sheet and pat into a rectangle about 7 by 9 in/17 by 23 cm. Wrap tightly with plastic and refrigerate for 1 hour.

When you begin the lamination process, the butter block and dough should be the same temperature: very cold. They will warm up quickly at room temperature, so working fast is very important. Remove the butter block rectangle from the refrigerator and, using a rolling pin dusted with a little bit of flour, roll it out just a little bit to make it more pliable. Lightly flour the surface in front of you and orient the butter block so the long side is facing you, and brush off any flour on the surface.

Remove the dough block from the fridge and place on top of the butter block so it is nearly flush with the right side of the butter block. Encase the dough in the butter block, as if closing a book, sealing the edges well. If the butter block is too cold to work with, let stand for a few moments on the counter and try again.

On a lightly floured surface, begin rolling the block until it is 12 by 18 in/30 by 20 cm. Brush any excess flour from the surface. Orient the rectangle so the long side is facing you, then fold the dough in thirds, like a business letter, squaring all the corners. Wrap tightly in plastic and refrigerate for about 1 hour.

Dust the surface of the dough and the work surface with flour, then roll the dough into a 12-by-24-in/20-by-60-cm rectangle, orient it again so the long side is facing you, and fold in both sides of the dough so that they meet in the middle, with a slight gap in between, then fold the two sides onto each other as if closing a book. Wrap in plastic and refrigerate for 30 minutes, then repeat this rolling and folding step one more time. Rewrap tightly in plastic and refrigerate until firm, at least 2 hours or up to overnight. At this point you can also portion the puff pastry for use in recipes by cutting it with a sharp knife. (If storing for future use, wrap tightly and freeze. It will keep for 1 month. Thaw in the refrigerator overnight before using.)

Yield: About 1 kg/2.2 lbs dough

PALMIERS

These extra-crispy sweet-and-salty bites are flavored with a slightly savory blend of aromatic seeds, and date sugar.

1 T fennel seeds

60 g/¼ cup white sesame seeds

1 T black sesame seeds

256 g/¾ cup date sugar

½ recipe Inverted Spelt Puff Pastry Dough (page 308), cold

28 g/2 T unsalted butter, melted

In a small sauté pan over medium-high heat, toast the fennel seeds until aromatic and lightly toasted, about 1 minute. Grind in a spice grinder or to a coarse texture with a mortar and pestle, then transfer to a small bowl.

In the now-empty sauté pan over medium-high heat, toast the white and black sesame seeds until lightly toasted and aromatic. Grind, then add to the fennel seeds. Measure 85 g/¼ cup of the date sugar into a small bowl and set aside.

On a lightly floured work surface, roll the dough into a 12-by-15-in/30-by-38-cm rectangle, orienting it so the long side is facing you. Mark the center of your dough, then make marks 2 in/5 cm in from both outside edges.

Brush the melted butter over the surface of the dough, dust with one-third of the remaining 170 g/½ cup sugar, then top with one-third of the toasted fennel and sesame seeds.

Fold in the left edge of the dough at the 2-in/5-cm mark you made, then repeat with the right side. Brush the newly exposed pieces of dough with half of the remaining butter and dust with half of the remaining sugar and fennel and sesame seeds as before. Fold in one more time, leaving one finger-width space in between the two columns of dough, and brush with the remaining butter and dust with the remaining sugar and fennel and sesame seeds.

Transfer to a parchment-lined baking sheet and refrigerate until cold enough to cut cleanly, at least 15 minutes or up to overnight. (The palmier dough can also be wrapped and frozen for up to 1 month. If freezing, transfer to the refrigerator to thaw the night before you plan to slice and bake the palmiers.)

Preheat the oven to 350°F/180°C. Arrange the dough on your work surface with the long side facing you. With a sharp knife, cut the dough into ¼-in/6-mm slices. Dip each palmier in the remaining 85 g/¼ cup date sugar, then set on parchment-lined baking sheets, spacing them about 2 in/5 cm apart.

Bake for 20 minutes, then remove the baking sheets from the oven and, using a spatula and working quickly, flip each palmier over. Return to the oven and bake for 5 minutes more. Remove from the oven and immediately transfer to a wire rack to let cool. These are best eaten the same day they are baked, but can be stored for up to 3 days in an airtight container.

Yield: Twelve large palmiers

PITHIVIER

The pithivier is a double-crusted free-form tart marrying two classic pastry base recipes, which we've reworked here. Spelt puff pastry is filled with pistachio frangipane. These two rich components are offset by tart cherries or apricots.

½ recipe Inverted Spelt Puff Pastry Dough (page 308)

340 g/1 cup Pistachio or Hazelnut Frangipane (page 325)

227 g/2 cups chopped, pitted cherries or apricots

EGG WASH

20 g/1 egg yolk

30 g/2 T heavy cream

40 g/2 T grade B maple syrup

Divide the puff pastry dough into two pieces, one slightly larger than the other, and refrigerate the smaller piece while you roll out the larger one. On a lightly floured surface, roll out the dough into a 10-in/25-cm round, rotating the dough to ensure even thickness and dusting beneath the dough with additional flour to prevent sticking. Remove the smaller piece of dough from the refrigerator and roll into a 9-in/23-cm round. Line a baking sheet with parchment and transfer one of the rounds of dough to the baking sheet, then top with a second piece of parchment and the second round of dough. Transfer to the refrigerator and chill 15 to 30 minutes.

Remove the smaller pastry circle from the refrigerator (still on the parchment), and top with the frangipane, using an offset spatula to spread the frangipane nearly to the edges, leaving a 1-in/2.5-cm border. Evenly scatter the cherries or apricots on top of the frangipane.

To make the egg wash: In a small bowl, whisk together the egg yolk and heavy cream until combined.

With a pastry brush, brush the exposed edge of the pastry with some of the egg wash, taking care that the egg wash does not drip over the edges of the pastry (which would seal the edge and prevent the dough from puffing).

Remove the larger pastry circle from the refrigerator and drape over the fruit. Beginning in the center and working your way out to the edges, lightly press air out of the surface of the pastry and press lightly to adhere the top and bottom pastry layers around the border. Cut a ½-in/12-mm circular vent hole in the center of the pastry to allow the steam to escape. Using the back of a butter knife draw decorative lines from the center of the pastry out to the edges, being careful to press lightly just to leave an indentation but not cut through the pastry layers. Brush the top with the remaining egg wash. Transfer the pithivier (still on the parchment) to a baking sheet, wrap the pan tightly with plastic, and freeze for at least 1 hour and up to overnight.

Preheat the oven to 350°F/180°C. Bake the pithivier pastry for 30 to 45 minutes, rotating the baking sheet halfway through baking to ensure even browning. Remove from the oven and brush with the maple syrup. Let cool completely, then cut into slices and serve.

Yield: One 9-in/22-cm pithivier

PAILLETTES

Our paillettes are strips of spelt puff pastry flavored with strong cheese and a za'atar-inspired mixture of seeds and aromatics, then twisted and baked to make enticing savory crisps.

1 T cumin seeds

1 T caraway seeds

1 T white sesame seeds

1 T poppy seeds

1 T anise seeds

1 t flaky sea salt, such as Maldon

1 t minced fresh thyme leaves

1 t ground black pepper

¼ t Hungarian paprika

½ recipe Inverted Spelt Puff Pastry Dough (page 308)

228 g/2 cups grated Gruyère cheese

In a small bowl, combine the cumin, caraway, sesame, poppy, and anise seeds, with the salt, thyme, pepper, and paprika.

On a lightly floured work surface with a lightly floured rolling pin, roll the puff pastry into a 6-by-12-in/15-by-30-cm rectangle. Orient the dough so that the long side is facing you, and distribute 114 g/1 cup of cheese over the left two-thirds of the dough. Cover with a clean piece of parchment paper. Roll the rolling pin over the parchment paper, pressing gently so that the cheese adheres to the dough. Remove the parchment paper and fold the dough in thirds, folding the right side (without the cheese) in first, like a business letter, squaring all the corners. Wrap well with plastic and refrigerate for 15 minutes. Line a baking sheet with parchment paper.

Remove the dough from the refrigerator, transfer to a lightly floured work surface and, with a lightly floured rolling pin, roll into a 8-by-12-in/20-by-30-cm rectangle. Distribute the remaining 114 g/1 cup of cheese across the surface of the dough, then top with the spice mix. Cover with a piece of parchment and roll the rolling pin over the parchment paper, pressing gently so that the cheese and spices adhere. Cut dough into twelve 1-by-8-in/2.5-by-20-cm strips. Twist the strips of dough at least twice. Transfer to the prepared baking sheet and press lightly on both ends to reinforce their shape. Freeze the paillettes until firm, at least 1 hour or up to overnight.

Preheat the oven to 350°F/180°C. Bake paillettes straight from freezer for 25 to 30 minutes, rotating the pans halfway through baking, the edges are puffed and deep golden brown. Serve warm or at room temperature. These are best eaten the same day they are baked.

Yield: Twelve 8-in/25-cm paillettes

FLAMMEKUCHEN

Flammekuchen is a simple savory Alsatian tart typically made with crème fraîche, bacon, and onions, which is sublime when these humble ingredients are combined with skill. The base of this tart is the hearty and flavorful Inverted Spelt Flour Puff Pastry. It's rolled very thin so the whole-grain pastry is not heavy after baking, then topped with crème fraîche, bacon, and sautéed leeks. In the springtime, I like to top these tarts fresh from the oven with bitter green flowering watercress and arugula blossoms. For a vegetarian version, top the tart before baking with blanched asparagus tossed in olive oil, green garlic, red pepper flakes, and shaved slices of Meyer lemon, and season with salt and freshly ground black pepper.

227 g/15 strips thick-cut bacon, cut crosswise into ¼-in/6-mm batons

300 g/3 leeks, white and light green parts only, thinly sliced

½ recipe Inverted Spelt Puff Pastry Dough (page 308)

120 g/½ cup Crème Fraîche (page 245)

142 g/1 cup shredded Comté or Gruyère cheese

20 g/2 T fresh chive blossoms or other edible flowers

In a small sauté pan over medium-high heat, add the bacon and cook, stirring, until crisp and brown, about 7 minutes. Remove the bacon from the pan with a slotted spoon and transfer to paper towels to drain.

Add the leeks to the pan, reduce the heat to low and cook, stirring frequently, until tender and just beginning to caramelize, about 15 minutes. Transfer the cooked leeks to a bowl and let cool.

Preheat the oven to 350°F/180°C. Roll the dough into a 13-by-9-in/33-by-23-cm rectangle about ⅛ in/4 mm thick and transfer to an unlined baking sheet. Prick the dough lightly with a fork to prevent it from swelling up during baking, leaving a ½-in/12-mm border on all sides. Transfer to the refrigerator or freezer until well chilled, 10 to 15 minutes.

Remove the dough from the refrigerator and, with an offset spatula, spread the crème fraîche on the chilled dough, leaving a ½-in/12-mm border on all sides. Top with the leeks, bacon, and cheese.

Bake for 30 to 35 minutes, rotating the baking sheet halfway through baking, until the pastry and cheese are golden brown and the edges are puffed (if the cheese is browning too quickly, tent the tart with aluminum foil). Remove from the oven and top with the chive blossoms, then transfer the tart to a wire rack to cool. Serve warm or at room temperature.

Yield: One 13-by-9-in/33-by-23-cm tart

GOLDEN BRIOCHE

Brioche typically has a rich yellow hue from the high percentage of eggs and butter that make up the dough. Starting with our basic natural-leaven brioche, here I've added a portion of whole-grain Kamut and semolina flours to the mix, adding more flavor and saturating the golden color. The addition of Kefir Butter brings a sharp note to balance the rich flavor, while conditioning the delicate dough, though any butter will work in this recipe. Brioche is technically a bread dough, but it's amply enriched with butter and eggs, and so far from the style of breads in part one of the book, that it seemed to fit more practically here in the pastry section. But because it is a bread dough, the measurements for this recipe are given in baker's percentages and grams.

	BAKER'S %	WEIGHT
Kefir Butter (see page 245) or unsalted butter	45	160 g
FLOUR		
Medium-strong wheat flour	35	123 g
Whole-grain Kamut flour	25	88 g
Whole-grain semolina flour	25	88 g
All-purpose flour	15	53 g
GRANULATED SUGAR	10	35 g
FINE SEA SALT	2.5	10 g
INSTANT YEAST	2	6 g
WET INGREDIENTS		
Eggs, at room temperature	35	125 g
Overnight Poolish (page 58)	35	125 g
Whole milk or buttermilk	21	75 g
Egg yolks	10	35 g
Leaven	25	90 g

EGG WASH

40 g/2 egg yolks

60 g/4 T heavy cream

About 30 minutes before you are ready to mix the brioche dough, remove the Kefir Butter from the refrigerator and let soften at room temperature until it is pliable but still cool.

In the bowl of a stand mixer fitted with a dough hook, combine the Kamut, semolina, and wheat flours with the sugar, salt, and yeast and mix to combine on low speed. Increase the speed to medium and add the eggs, poolish, milk, egg yolks, and leaven, scraping down the bowl with a rubber spatula as needed. Turn the mixer off and let the dough rest in the bowl for 15 to 20 minutes.

After the dough has rested, mix it on medium-high speed until it releases from the sides of the bowl, 6 to 8 minutes. This indicates that the dough is sufficiently developed to begin incorporating the butter. Make sure the butter is soft and pliable but still cool and not melted.

Cut the Kefir Butter into ½-in/12-mm pieces. With the mixer on medium speed, add the pieces of butter, one at a time, to the middle of the bowl where the dough hook meets the dough. Continue until the butter is incorporated. The dough will be silky smooth and homogenous, with no visible bits of butter.

Transfer the dough to a bowl and set in a cool place (70°F/20°C) for 2 hours for the bulk fermentation. During the first hour, give the dough two turns, following the folding and turning instructions on page 38. During the second hour, give it one turn. This is a very forgiving dough. If you want to shape the dough the next day, place the dough in a freezer-proof container after the 2-hour bulk fermentation and freeze for 3 to 5 hours, then transfer to the refrigerator and store overnight. If you are shaping the dough and baking the brioche the same day, make sure that the bulk fermentation occurs in a cool place, or the butter will melt out of the dough and the dough will feel greasy.

Just before shaping the dough, grease two 9-by-5-in/23-by-13-cm loaf pans. Use a dough spatula to pull the dough from the bowl onto an unfloured work surface. With a bench knife, cut the dough into two equal pieces. Shape each piece of dough into a round and place seam-side down into the prepared pans.

Place each piece of dough in a pan and let rise in a draft-free place at warm room temperature (75°F/24°C) for 1½ to 2 hours.

Preheat the oven to 450°F/230°C.

To make the egg wash: In a small bowl, whisk together the egg yolks and heavy cream.

Using a pastry brush, brush the top of each loaf with the egg wash. Bake until golden brown, 35 to 40 minutes. Unmold and let cool on a wire rack. Store for up to 2 days, wrapped in plastic.

Yield: Makes 1 kg/2.2 lb dough; enough for two 9-in/23-cm loaves

Butter for greasing pans

85 g/½ cup maple sugar

1 recipe Golden Brioche dough (see page 318)

EGG WASH

20 g/1 egg yolk

30 g/2 T heavy cream

40 g/2 T grade B maple syrup

MAPLE SUGAR–GLAZED BRIOCHE

Brushing the insides of the pans or molds with melted butter and then coating them with maple sugar before baking will glaze the brioche crust during baking, adding a slight sweetness and the aroma of maple syrup.

Grease two 9-by-5-in/23-by-13-cm loaf pans with butter, then generously dust with maple sugar, dividing evenly. Portion the dough into four pieces and roll each piece into a ball.

Transfer two balls into each of the prepared pans and let rise in a draft-free place at warm room temperature (75°F/24°C) for 1½ to 2 hours. Preheat the oven to 450°F/230°C.

To make the egg wash: In a small bowl, whisk together the egg yolk and heavy cream.

Brush the egg wash on the surface of both loaves and bake until golden brown, 35 to 40 minutes. With a pastry brush, brush the tops of each with maple syrup, then unmold onto a wire rack and let cool completely. Store, for up to 2 days, wrapped in plastic.

Yield: Two 9-by-5-in/23-by-13-cm loaves

BRIOCHE SMOKED POTATO BUNS

This bread was inspired by a chef friend who asked me to riff on Joël Robuchon's *pain au lait* recipe. We workshopped a leaven brioche flavored with smoked potatoes, an ingredient always on hand at Bar Tartine. Presented here is the basic technique, which makes an epic griddled burger bun. Laminating this dough with additional butter to make small pull-apart loaves yields a petit pain for the ages.

Generous 2 handfuls alderwood chips
120 g/1 medium Yukon gold potato
½ recipe Golden Brioche dough
(page 318)

EGG WASH
20 g/1 egg yolk
15 g/1 T heavy cream

Preheat the oven to 350°F/180°C. Place the alderwood chips in a heavy-bottomed lidded cast-iron pot or wok. Set the pot over high heat until the chips have begun to smoke, about 5 minutes.

Rinse the potato and prick all over with a fork. Place a steamer basket over the smoking chips and put the potato into the basket. Cover with the lid, transfer the pot to the oven, and bake until a fork pierces the potato easily, 45 minutes to 1 hour. Remove from the oven and let cool, then cut into the potato pieces and pass through a ricer, skin and all.

Put the brioche dough in the bowl of a stand mixer fitted with the paddle attachment. Add the cooked, cooled potato to the dough and mix on low speed until the potato has broken up and is well combined with the dough.

When you are ready to shape the buns, line a baking sheet with parchment paper. Cut the dough into 6 pieces, each about 115 g. Form each piece of dough into a bun shape. Place the buns on the baking sheet, spacing them at least 6 in/15 cm apart. Press slightly to flatten them a bit. Let rise at moderate room temperature (68 to 72°F/20 to 22°C) for 1½ to 2 hours. Preheat the oven to 450°F/230°C.

To make the egg wash: In a small bowl, add the egg yolk and heavy cream and whisk to combine.

Brush each bun with egg wash. Bake for 15 minutes, until golden brown. Remove from the oven and transfer to a wire rack to let cool. Store, for up to 2 days, wrapped in plastic.

Yield: Six buns

BOSTOCK

Bostock, or twice-baked brioche, has been one of my favorite preparations using brioche since my first taste of it in Paris two decades ago. Here is a whole-food version of the classic, using our Golden Brioche. The simple syrup used to moisten the toasted brioche is made with citrus juice and zest, honey, and orange liqueur.

ORANGE SYRUP

227 g/1 cup fresh orange juice

114 g/½ cup Cointreau or other orange liqueur

40 g/2 T buckwheat honey

Zest of 3 oranges

8 slices Golden Brioche (page 318), each about ½ in/12 mm thick, toasted, crusts removed

340 g/1 cup orange marmalade, apricot jam, or berry jam

680 g/3 cups Pistachio Frangipane (page 325)

114 g/1 cup sliced almonds

Powdered sugar for dusting

Preheat the oven to 400°F/200°C.

To make the orange syrup: In a small bowl, combine the orange juice, Cointreau, honey, and orange zest.

Arrange the brioche toasts on a baking sheet and, using a pastry brush, thoroughly brush with the orange syrup until they are very moist; use all the syrup.

Spread each brioche toast with a layer of marmalade, dividing it evenly, and top with a ¼-in/6-mm thick layer of frangipane. Top with the almonds, dividing evenly.

Bake for 15 to 20 minutes until deep golden brown. The frangipane will caramelize and the almonds will toast. Transfer to a wire rack and let cool. Dust with powdered sugar just before serving. Bostock is best eaten the day it is made.

Yield: Eight pieces

PISTACHIO FRANGIPANE

115 g/1 cup powdered sugar

115 g/½ cup unsalted butter, at room temperature

70 g/⅔ cup chopped raw pistachios

50 g/1 large egg, at room temperature

20 g/1 egg yolk, at room temperature

10 g/1 T plus 1 t cornstarch

188 g/¾ cup Nut Milk Pastry Cream (page 327), made with Pistachio Nut Milk (page 326), at room temperature

Pinch of fine sea salt

Zest of 1 lemon

20 g/1 T plus 1 t Cointreau or other orange liqueur (optional)

Sift the powdered sugar into the bowl of a stand mixer fitted with the paddle attachment. Add the butter and beat on low speed to combine. Increase the speed to medium and beat until smooth and creamy. Stop the mixer and scrape down the bowl with a rubber spatula. Add the pistachios, egg, egg yolk, cornstarch, pastry cream, salt, lemon zest, and Cointreau (if using) and beat on low speed until all the ingredients are evenly incorporated, stopping to scrape down the bowl as needed. The mixture may have a slightly "broken" appearance, which is normal. This will keep, for up to 2 days, refrigerated.

Yield: 680 g/3 cups

HAZELNUT FRANGIPANE VARIATION

Replace the raw pistachios with chopped skinned raw hazelnuts and use pastry cream made with hazelnut nut milk. In place of the Cointreau, use brandy.

PISTACHIO NUT MILK

Our foray into nut milks was one of our more challenging experiments. We wanted milks that were creamy and richly infused with nut flavor, and that could be used to make nut-based pastry creams. After tireless experimentation using all different nuts, we finally settled on some favorites. Pistachios, which yield a green milk, are especially delicious. Hazelnuts, almonds, and cashews also make an excellent nut milk.

226 g/1¾ cups plus 2 T raw pistachios
680 g/3 cups cow's milk or water
30 g/2 T sugar
¼ t fine sea salt

Put the nuts in a large glass or stainless-steel bowl or food-safe container and add water to cover by 2 in/5 cm. Let soak in a cool place overnight or up to 24 hours.

Rinse the soaked nuts in a fine-mesh sieve under cool water. In a blender, blend the nuts and milk (or water) on high speed. Continue blending until smooth, 2 to 3 minutes. Add the sugar and salt and blend 30 seconds longer. The nut milk will keep, for up to 5 days, refrigerated. Shake well before drinking or using in a recipe.

Yield: 912 g/4 cups

FAVORITE NUT MILK VARIATIONS

Hazelnut Nut Milk: Substitute 226 g/1½ cups plus 1 T raw hazelnuts for the pistachios.

Almond Nut Milk: Substitute 226 g/1½ cups plus 1 T raw almonds for the pistachios.

Cashew Nut Milk: Substitute 226 g/2 cups raw cashews for the pistachios.

NUT MILK PASTRY CREAM

Nut milks are refreshing on their own, but we typically use them to make pastry creams to fill éclairs and tarts. For a thicker nut milk with a viscosity more like heavy cream, use half as much water or milk as called for.

500 g/2 cups Pistachio Nut Milk (facing page)

¼ t fine sea salt

115 g/½ cup granulated sugar

20 g /3 T cornstarch

100 g/2 large eggs

55 g/4 T unsalted butter, at room temperature

Set a fine-mesh sieve over a large bowl and set aside. Pour the nut milk into a heavy saucepan. Add the salt, place over medium heat, and bring to just under a boil, stirring occasionally.

In a medium bowl, whisk together the sugar and cornstarch. Add the eggs and whisk until smooth.

Slowly ladle about one-third of the hot nut milk into the egg mixture, whisking constantly. Pour the egg-milk mixture into the saucepan containing the remaining hot nut milk and continue whisking over medium heat until it is as thick as lightly whipped cream, about 2 minutes.

(In order for the cornstarch to cook and thicken fully, the mixture must come just to the boiling point. However, if the cream is allowed to boil vigorously, it will curdle.)

Remove the cream from the heat and immediately pour through the sieve into the bowl. Using a rubber spatula, press the cream through the sieve, discarding any solids. Let cool for 10 minutes, stirring occasionally to prevent a skin from forming, until it reaches about 140°F/60°C on an instant-read thermometer.

Cut the butter into 30-g/1-tablespoon pieces. Whisk into the pastry cream, one piece at a time, always whisking until smooth before adding the next.

Cover the bowl with plastic, pressing directly onto the top of the cream (this prevents a skin from forming on the surface), transfer to the refrigerator, and refrigerate until cold. The pastry cream will keep, well covered, for up to 5 days, in the refrigerator.

Yield: 625 g/2½ cups

Select Photo Index

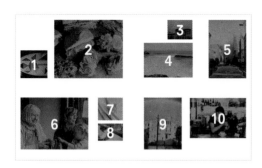

Pages 16–17

1. Andreini Serena Pintail Vaquero; 2. Bar Tartine lunch; 3. Valencia Street; 4. Left at OBSF; 5. SOMA; 6. Marianne, Liz, and Archer at Bar Tartine; 7. Back door on 18th street; 8. Front window facing Guerrero Street; 9. View from the Mill; 10. Nellie's capp in a white cup

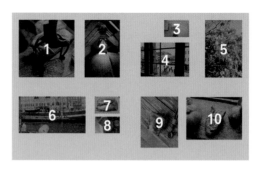

Pages 76–77

1. Slicing rugbrød; 2. Per's malting room; 3. Traveling to Copenhagen; 4. View from Royal Copenhagen HQ; 5. Quince blossoms; 6. Copenhagen harbor; 7. Mackeral with roe; 8. The real René's rye; 9. Herring and rhubarb on rye at Kille's; 10. Seeded bread at Camilla's

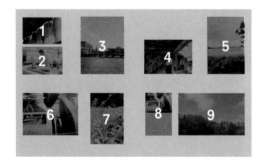

Pages 98–99

1. Grain silos; 2. Martin at Mathias Dahlgren; 3. Stockholm; 4. First week at Isa, Brooklyn, New York; 5. View from Kille's; 6. Sorting grain; 7. Wild ramps; 8. Ignacio at Isa; 9. Front window at Valhalla; 10. Fishing cabin across from the mill

Image numbers 2 and 8 courtesy of The Selby.

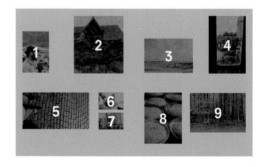

Pages 154–155

1. At Brotfest, Rauris, Austria; 2. Sonnenhausen, Germany; 3. Brassica napus; 4. View from Sonnen-hausen; 5. Alpine wood block; 6. Whole-grain bread in Rauris; 7. Berlin, Gendarmenmarkt Konzerthaushall, Berlin; 8. Bread rising at Rauris; 9. View while driving from Berlin to Poland

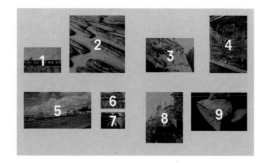

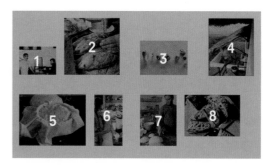

Pages 196–197

1. Paris street; 2. Patrick's baguettes, Boulangerie des Îles, Brittany; 3. Statue of a winged lion, Fontaine Saint-Michel in Paris; 4. Du Pain et des Idées, Paris; 5. View from the Paris-Brittany TGV; 6. Patrick's croissants; 7. Liz in Provence; 8. Notre Dame cathedral in Paris; 9. Pain Poilâne

Pages 230–231

1. Gentile and Muller, Zihuatenejo; 2. Augustina, preparing rock fish; 3. Charlie's shells; 4. La casa; 5. *Pan Integral*; 6. Siesta prep; 7. Preshaped bread; 8. *Pan Integral*, baked

Acknowledgments

Tartine Book No. 3 would not have been possible without the support of so many people in the Tartine universe, past and present. Special thanks to my wife and partner, Elisabeth, and our daughter, Archer, for enduring and encouraging the process. The dedicated work of my team at the bakery, led by Melissa Roberts in the pastry kitchen and Lori Oyamada on bread, along with Vinny Eng, Suzanne Yacovetti, Sierra Zumwalt, and Tahlia Harbour for managing the cafe, has enabled me to travel, learn, and bring new ideas back for us to develop. Inspiration from chef friends at home, Nick Balla and Cortney Burns of Bar Tartine, other chefs in the Bay Area, and abroad, continues to drive me to learn, improve, and push creativity at home.

Thanks to Katherine Cowles's unwavering advocacy, Jessica Battilana's editorial direction, and the collaborative testing and development of recipes by Richard Hart and Laurie Ellen Pellicano, we were able to freely explore new ideas over the course of the entire project. Chronicle Books' impressive effort to finally wrap this up was led by Lorena Jones's intrepid and remarkable work.

Juliette Cezzar knew exactly what I wanted after our first conversation. Special thanks to her for continuing to know, even as I kept changing it until the end, and for sweating the details with conviction.

INDEX

A

Acme Bread Company, 13, 199
Agrologica, 20
Almonds
    Bostock, 322
    Chocolate-Rye Tart, 292–95
    Croquant d'Amandes, 246
    Lemon Poppy Kefir Pound Cake, 277–78
    Nut Milk, 326
    Nut Milk Pastry Cream, 327
    Oat Porridge bread, 178
Amaranth, 29
    Sprouted Amaranth bread, 128
Amazake, 146
    Purple Barley Amazake bread, 146
    Sprouted Buckwheat-Einkorn bread, 150
Amylase, 23
Andersson, Fredrik, 101
Apples
    Apple-Walnut Tea Cake, 274
    Bohemian Apple Layer Cake, 287–89
    Buckwheat-Apple Tart, 297–99
Apricots
    Bostock, 322
    Chocolate-Rye Tart, 292–95
    Pithivier, 312–13
Aurion, 20
Austria. *See* Germany and Austria, baking in
Autolyse, 21, 23, 37

B

Bacon
    Flammekuchen, 316
Baguettes, Spelt and Toasted Corn Flour, 59–63
Baker's percentages, 24
Baking, 41
Baldwin Hill Bakery, 200
Balla, Nick, 54, 108, 188
Banana Tea Cake, 276
Barley, 27
    Barley Porridge–Flaxseed bread, 180
    Barley-Walnut-Fig Cookies, 253–54
    Cheddar Cheese Sablés, 262–63
    Purple Barley Amazake bread, 146
    Sprouted Purple Barley bread, 114
    sprouting, 110
    Toasted Barley bread, 144
Basic (organic food markets), 158
Bech, Bo, 103, 104–5, 241
Beer
    lambics, 234–35
    Purple Barley Amazake bread, 146
    René's Rye bread, 140
    René-Style Crispbreads, 216
    Sprouted Buckwheat-Einkorn bread, 150

Sprouted Emmer with Maple and Beer bread, 134
    Toasted Barley bread, 144
Bench rest, 39
Berg, Martin, 102–5
Berg, Stefan, 102–3, 105, 214
Bergamot
    Bergamot Syrup, 284–86
    Buckwheat, Bergamot, and Blood Orange Chiffon Cake, 284–86
Berkshire Mountain Bakery, 92, 166, 194
Berries
    Bostock, 322
    Fruit Scones, 279–81
Blue Cheese Sablés, 263
Bolvig, René, 108, 140
Borgen, Anders, 20
Bostock, 322
Boulangerie du Pain et des Idées, 59
Boulangerie Savoyarde, Le, 158
Bourdon, Richard, 31, 46, 66, 92, 144, 159, 160, 166, 186, 188, 194, 201–3, 240
Bras, Michel, 224
Bread Alone, 199
Breads. *See also* Brioche; Cracked and flaked grain breads; Crispbreads; Porridge breads; Seeded breads; Sprouted grain hearth loaves; Sprouted grain pan loaves
    Buckwheat with Toasted Groats and Crème Fraîche, 54–55
    desem, 198–201, 203
    Emmer/Einkorn, 72
    French, 23, 59–60
    Kamut 60%, 68
    master method for, 32, 34–41
    Spelt and Toasted Corn Flour Baguettes, 59–63
    Spelt-Wheat, 74
    Wheat–Rye 10%, 50
    Wheat–Rye 20%, 52
    White-Wheat Blend (Ode to Bourdon), 46
Brioche
    Bostock, 322
    Brioche Smoked Potato Buns, 321
    Golden Brioche, 318–19
    Maple Sugar–Glazed Brioche, 320
Brot and Butter, 160
Brown Rice Porridge bread, 186
Buckwheat, 28
    Buckwheat-Apple Tart, 297–99
    Buckwheat, Bergamot, and Blood Orange Chiffon Cake, 284–86
    Buckwheat-Hazelnut Sablés, 261
    Buckwheat-Nori Crispbreads, 218
    Buckwheat Pâte Sucrée, 299–300
    Buckwheat Tart with Honey-Lemon Cream, 299–301
    Buckwheat with Toasted Groats and Crème Fraîche bread, 54–55
    Sprouted Buckwheat bread, 132
    Sprouted Buckwheat–Einkorn bread, 150
    sprouting, 110
Buco, Il, 100
Buns, Brioche Smoked Potato, 321
Burns, Courtney, 188